The Book on Private Money

Adam J. Davis

How to Get the Cash from Private Investors to Fund Your Real Estate Deals

"With the materials from your course and your help, I was able to secure $100,000 in Private Money less than 7 days after your seminar! Thank you!"
                              Larry Armstrong
                              Fort Gratiot MI

"I wanted to thank you for your presentation…With your quick wit and humor you captured everyone's attention and your presentation was an inspiration to us and the rest of the audience. It explained in your own easy style how anyone can adopt your business philosophy with immediate success cultivating investors, acquiring other peoples' money and improving their business."
                              Daniel Lello
                          KM Capital Management
                              Cincinnati, OH

"Hi Adam, We had a wonderful time learning your techniques in raising private money…it is wonderful to learn knew things. Most of all we thank you from our hearts that you are willing to help us to achieve our goals in life."
                                      Tim G
                                Port Huron, MI

"Thanks to your techniques and materials, I was able to secure my first private investor and do my first rehab deal within two weeks. I highly recommend Adam Davis' private money training to anyone who wants to make money in real estate."
                              Chris Paglialunga
                        Urban Property Development
                        www.RehabsDoneRight.com

None of the information anywhere in this book is meant as legal or tax advice. The content of this book is offered as information only. Persons reading this book and any supplementary materials are encouraged to seek independent counsel for advice regarding their individual legal or tax issues.

Some resources contained in this book are from websites not maintained by Adam J. Davis, and he therefore is not responsible for their content. Adam J. Davis makes no guarantee or warranty, express or implied, concerning this book, nor does he make any guarantees or warrantees concerning other materials/information to which this book refers.

© 2010 Adam J. Davis
All Rights Reserved.

No part of this publication may be reproduced, stored in a retrieval system, or transmitted, in any form or by any means, electronic, mechanical, photocopying, recording, or otherwise, without the written permission of the author.

First published by Dog Ear Publishing
4010 W. 86th Street, Ste H
Indianapolis, IN 46268
www.dogearpublishing.net

ISBN: 978-160844-430-4

This book is printed on acid-free paper.

Printed in the United States of America

Acknowledgments

This book is dedicated to: my wife, Rebecca and my son, Isaac. Thank you for your love, support and understanding. And also my parents, for always encouraging me to pursue my dreams.

Special thanks to: Kendal Davis, Julia Mayes and DC for making this book a reality. I couldn't have done it without your help.

With appreciation to: my business partners, Nathan Mayes and Dylan Tanaka – thank you for being great partners and friends.

Table of Contents

Part I – Changing the Game 1
    Chapter 1 –   The 'Holy Grail' of Real Estate Investing 5
    Chapter 2 –   Why Should They Invest With *You*? 19

Part II – Private Money Attraction Principles 25
    Chapter 3 –   Private Money Attraction Principle #1 26
    Chapter 4 –   Private Money Attraction Principle #2 32
    Chapter 5 –   Private Money Attraction Principle #3 37
    Chapter 6 –   Private Money Attraction Principle #4 40
    Chapter 7 –   Private Money Attraction Principle #5 42

Part III – How to Get Private Investors 45
    Chapter 8 –   KISS 49
    Chapter 9 –   How to Push Investors Your Way 62
    Chapter 10 – How to Pull Investors Toward You 68

Part IV – Seal the Deal 83
    Chapter 11 – Getting the Meeting 85
    Chapter 12 – Presenting the Deal 92
    Chapter 13 – What Rate of Return Should You Pay? 105
    Chapter 14 – Closing the Deal 109

Part V – Other Important Things with Private Money 115
    Chapter 15 – What Not to Do 116
    Chapter 16 – Private Money Goldmine 120
    Chapter 17 – Taxes 127
    Chapter 18 – Securities Laws 132

Final Thoughts 141

Bonus Chapter #1 – Using the 'Other Half" of
                           Your Investing Brain 143

Bonus Chapter #2 – The Goose That Laid the Golden Eggs 152

PART I

Changing the Game

What you're about to read may change the way you view real estate investing forever. When you finish this book, you'll be equipped with the knowledge you need to fund any deal at any time and build a lucrative real estate investing business – *without* having to rely on banks, mortgage companies, hard money lenders or lines of credit. If you've already experienced some success in real estate, after reading this book you'll have the confidence and tools to do more deals, bigger projects and propel yourself to the next level.

Once upon a time, I thought I had it all figured out. After getting my college degree and a nice job offer, I went into corporate finance. A brief stint on the corporate ladder pushed me into starting my own business. I wanted to be my own boss, to have true financial security. Real estate was going to be my key to wealth. Financial freedom was just around the corner! Having worked in the financial industry, I thought with my knowledge, good credit and creativity that no deal was beyond my reach.

Boy, was I in for a rude awakening!

Shortly after I left my full time job, I found out that cash was the currency that went the furthest in real estate investing. As much as my creative deals worked to acquire properties, I still needed money to rehab houses and cash for down payments on bigger projects. After having what felt like a few hundred pounds of sand kicked in my face, I realized I needed an edge. The market was demanding it. I was faced with an uncomfortable ultimatum: get a hold of some serious cash or get out of real estate. Thus began my private money journey.

Over the years, I've been privileged to work and invest in different markets, transact many different types of deals and do business with people from all walks of life. Through these rich and diverse experiences, I have developed and refined principles, techniques and methods for raising money from individual private investors to finance all or part of every single real estate transaction that I complete.

Using none of my own money, I have closed millions of dollars in real estate, done hundreds of deals and piled up tens of thousands of dollars per month in cash flow in my businesses. Equally as important, my private investors have profited quite handsomely. What you will read in this book will help you do the same thing; no matter what your education is, no matter how much experience you have nor how much cash you have in the bank right now. The principles and techniques you will learn will work for every market segment and deal type, from the $50,000 home rehab to the $5,000,000 shopping mall.

This book will shave off years of frustration and unfulfilled dreams and prevent millions of dollars worth of mistakes. You'll learn how to create new investment opportunities and attract private money *immediately*.

Breaking Down Barriers
The amount of *mis*information that exists about private money is frightening. Private money seems to be a very mysterious, almost mythical thing to many real estate investors. It shouldn't be this way.

I'll never forget the time several years ago when I was hosting a workshop on how to finance real estate deals and a gentleman in the front row shifted nervously in his seat and raised his hand. He proceeded to ask me how he could get private money. I replied by asking him what type of deals he wanted to do. He replied that he wanted to purchase apartment buildings. Curious, I then asked him what real estate experience he had and he told me that he had owned a large apartment building for the better part of 20 years and had done some single family house investing as well.

Impressed by this, I asked him how he had been financing his property purchases. He replied that he had simply saved up his cash flow and then bought houses using mortgages, often with large down payments. He then told me he was almost paralyzed by inaction because he had no idea where to begin looking for private money and didn't know how to set up or propose a deal to an investor.

I was shocked. How could it be that a guy who had been profitably investing in real estate for over 20 years had *absolutely no idea* about private money? That was just the beginning. In the months and years since my eye-opening experience that day at my seminar, I have talked to hundreds of real estate investors who feel that private money is unreachable or unattainable. Some think there is a secret or conspiracy preventing them from getting private money. Nothing could be further from the truth. I want to break down all of these myths and misperceptions and show you how to tap into the vast resources of private investors.

Successful real estate investing comes down to a few basic elements, and financing is one of them. For several years, I've conducted private money education seminars and counseled hundreds of investors. Thousands of conversations later, I'm convinced of this: long-term success in real estate comes down to getting the best deals at the best prices — with the best financing. I am also convinced that private money is the ultimate "X" factor that can mean the difference between a net worth of $2,000,000 and a net worth of $200,000,000.

Markets evolve over time. Deals come and go. But in the long run, having the ability to close any deal at any time is the best way to build real estate wealth. And for savvy real estate investors, the potential of private money is *limitless*. This book will show you how to acquire more private money than you ever thought possible. It will expand your reality and bring even your most lofty goals within reach.

There is one thing that I request of you before you read beyond this point: you must commit to a 'detoxification' of all preexisting junk, myths and roadblocks you may currently have about private money. You simply won't be able to learn and implement the valuable information I have to share if you bring old baggage along.

In this spirit, please repeat the following after me:

- It doesn't matter what my background is…
- It doesn't matter what my education level is…
- It doesn't matter what type of deals I want to do…
- It doesn't matter what my personality type is…

I CAN and WILL have private investors fund my real estate investments.

Remember, if you don't believe in yourself, chances are nobody else will. As you'll see in the coming chapters, this is a critical aspect of winning the great game of real estate using other people's money.

You'll have a lot of fun reading this book, you're going to learn a lot and, most importantly, you'll get *results*. Let's Rock n' Roll….

Chapter 1

The 'Holy Grail' of Real Estate Investing

Most people are attracted to real estate investing by dreams of great riches. Wealth through real estate is accessible to everyone, at one level or another, and as a result, almost anyone with ambition and a little knowledge can become an investor overnight. Yet, sadly, few investors hang on long enough to achieve the financial success they dream of. Why?

The reason is: most investors operate from a position of *unconscious incompetence* — they don't know what they don't know. And one of the most critical things they don't know is this: Private money is the *Holy Grail* of real estate investing.

What is Private Money?
There are many misconceptions floating around in the marketplace about what "private money" is. The simple definition is:

> *Money an individual person invests with you in exchange for a return on that investment*

Before we drill down into the intricacies of what private money *is*, let's clarify what private money is *not*...

Private Money is Not "Hard Money"
Many investors operate under the assumption that there's no difference between hard money and private money. Not true! Hard money lenders are individuals or companies who are in the business of providing short-term acquisition and rehab financing for real estate investments. While it *is* true that both hard money and private money can come from private individuals, let's take a closer look at the differences between the two:

Figure 1.1

	Private Money	Hard Money
Private Money vs. Hard Money		
Points (up front interest)	No	Yes
High Interest Rate	No	Yes
Rehab Draws	No	Yes
Mandatory Refinancing	No	Yes
Short Term	Sometimes	Yes
Senior Lien	Sometimes	Yes
Reliable	Yes	No

One of the big drawbacks of hard money is its inflexibility. There is little margin for error when using a hard money loan. You'll always be constrained by the lender's requirements. How do I know this? Because *I* make hard money loans. That's right: I accumulate private money from investors, and when I have a few extra hundred grand in the bank, I will lend that money to other real estate investors. But, I have *very* strict rules. I make sure the person I'm lending to is ultra-credit worthy and has plenty of real estate experience. And, borrowing money from me is *very* expensive. In other words, most people won't qualify for my hard money loans.

Now, the fact that I won't lend money to a particular person doesn't mean they can't qualify for a loan elsewhere, or that they won't make money on the deal. But to investors who don't qualify for a hard money loan, I always offer one piece of advice: *Get private money.* Private money cures all ills. With a private lender or partner, you can simply pull the trigger when the right deal comes along, instead of being forced to shop it around with the hope of securing a hard money loan or mortgage, which can be like trying to find a needle in a haystack.

Another painful reality of hard money loans is the thousands of dollars that you will flush down the toilet in unnecessary points and interest. And, to add insult to injury, most hard money lenders will charge fees and points before you ever pick up a hammer on the rehab.

Let's go through an example of how relying on hard money can really crush your bottom line: Assume you're going to buy, fix and flip a property and you have a three-month time frame for completing the deal — from purchase to sale. Here is what you'd be looking at with a typical hard money loan:

Figure 1.2

Hard Money Loan	
Loan amount	$150,000
Loan Term	3 Months
Interest Rate	12%
Points Paid	$4,500/3 pts
Interest Paid	$4,500
Total Cost of Funds	**$9,000**

Now, lets say you had a private money loan for the same amount, at a 10% interest rate:

Figure 1.3

Private Money Loan	
Loan amount	$150,000
Loan Term	3 Months
Interest Rate	10%
Points Paid	$0
Interest Paid	$3,750
Total Cost of Funds	**$3,750**

Here's how the difference in financing costs looks after this deal:

Total Cost of Hard money: $9,000
Total Cost of Private money: $3,750
Difference: $5,250

If you were to flip 4 houses per year like the example above, you're literally throwing away *$21,000 in profits* by using hard money instead of private money! What could you do with an extra $21,000 per year? I, for one, would rather take a couple more nice, sun-soaked beach vacations!

Is hard money ever "good money" to use? Maybe. In a rare circumstance if you just don't have the cash and the deal is too sweet to pass up, hard money could be a solution. But, if you had a cash horde of private money, you wouldn't need to give a hard money lender the time of day!

Oh, and one more thing about hard money…
If you rely on hard money financing, you'll almost certainly lose deals to cash buyers backed by private money — and you'll lose out *often*. For instance, if you're pursuing bank-owned properties, you'll find that banks and other asset managers won't be inclined to wait around for your loan approval. And you may not even be able to get a loan approval for the full amount you need to close and do the rehab.

You can now see why it's so critical to quickly build a roster of private investors. Never let your profits — or your company's future — be governed by the strict and often capricious criteria imposed by hard money lenders. You'll leave far too much money on the table — we're talking *thousands* on every deal. And that's money you'd be pocketing, if you had just one private investor. Think about it. Just one private investor! Private Money = Bigger Profit. And no headaches!

Mortgage Madness
If you've ever had to endure the labyrinthine mortgage process, you probably agree that it's about as much fun as a root canal. Environmental activist groups should be protesting banks and mortgage companies because of all the trees they kill with their mountains of paperwork. But, even though the process was a drag, you could still get mortgage financing for most investment properties a few years ago. All you had to do was come up with the down payment (which was where a private investor came in handy).

Then the game changed…

The mortgage market crashed. The tentacles of the sub-prime meltdown gripped the great ship of the economy like a giant squid, dragging it down, down, down. Suddenly, my favorite mortgage brokers were nowhere to be found — they were running for cover. The grand and glorious headlines about "the booming real estate market" were a thing of the past. The bubble had burst, and the media headlines became something else entirely. *Housing prices continue to drop. Economy in the grip of a mortgage meltdown...*

Seller financing and other buying techniques evaporated as home equity values shrank. My deal pipeline started to slow — what was once a steady stream slowed to a trickle. Banks and mortgage companies left many real estate investors holding the bag. Promises were made but not kept. To add insult to injury, it wasn't long before business pundits and government officials began to blame all the mortgage market woes on real estate investors! It was shameful to blame the entrepreneurs for the crisis, but, I digress...

―――――――――――――$$$$ Resource $$$$―――――――――――――
Learn more about creative financing with Private Money.
Sign up for the free 10 week email course at
www.TheBookonPrivateMoney.com.
―――――――――――――$$$$$$―――――――――――――

Right now, it's extremely difficult (if not impossible in some parts of the country), to purchase distressed real estate with a mortgage. For both residential and commercial properties, the banks and mortgage companies that have managed to survive (most were tossed a lifeline from Uncle Sam) are puckered up so tight you couldn't blast a loan out of their hands with a stick of dynamite. The mortgage process, even now, for traditional real estate purchases (such as homeowner to homeowner) is like navigating a treacherous mountain pass — one small slip-up and the deal goes bye-bye. Forever. And, if you think the 'go-go' days of cheap mortgage money will return soon, think again. Uncle Sam's hands are wrapped around the throat of the mortgage industry, with no sign of letting go anytime soon.

As an investor, if you're counting on big, government bailed-out institutions to finance your investments — you're inviting disaster. If I had a nickel for every time I've seen a real estate investor lose a deal because the mortgage company balked, or the shoddy bank appraisal came in too low, I'd be writing this book from my private island in Fiji.

Why Overpay if You Don't Have To?
If you're making purchase offers on distressed properties (where most of the good deals are) contingent on mortgage financing, you may be paying 15% – 20% too much on every single deal. Over time, this adds up to *thousands of dollars* in lost profits, and shoves your business goals much farther out of reach. Why?

Think about it: why would the bank take a big discount on their asking price for an REO property if they can't be absolutely *certain* the deal will close? The bank would be taking their property off the market (which could cost them a sure buyer) only to wait.... and wait... and wait...and wait for you to secure a mortgage. Plus, the bank whose property you are buying knows full well that the mortgage you applied for may not even close due to some obscure technicality, or simply because the loan approval officer is having a bad day. And, most importantly, the banks you're seeking financing from may well be in the same boat as the bank who's trying to unload foreclosure properties — *broke*! Your bank or mortgage company isn't going to be overly eager to finance a house that a fellow bank just took a bath on.

Now, let's say by some miracle you manage to get approved for some purchase money mortgages and close a few deals. Since there's a limit to the number of mortgages you can hold for investment properties (currently it's 4 or 5, depending on the whims of our friends at the mortgage companies and government agencies), your profits are pinched. I don't know about you, but I like the idea of having more than 4 or 5 properties in my portfolio. Even if you only want to flip or wholesale houses, you'll still feel the pinch. In other words, your business growth will be severely limited by forces beyond your control. Definitely *not* the path to achieving financial freedom and accumulating wealth, is it?

When this whole mortgage mess started, my lines of credit and financing options evaporated in the blink of an eye. At the time, I had no choice but to drum up more private money to keep my business afloat and profitable. Up to this point, I had used private money solely for down payments and rehab funding, but I moved quickly to fill my coffers with more private investors. Honestly, I had no other options.

I don't mind telling you: It's fun to drive by a bank and literally thumb your nose at their hollow "low interest mortgage" offers! After you start piling up your own private money, you'll have fun doing the same thing.

Two Sides of the Private Money Coin
Most of us have been conditioned to believe that "investing" is largely about Wall Street — stocks, bonds, mutual funds. But that's only part of the story. Under the surface of our free enterprise system, private money makes the business world go 'round.

Private money investing is a multibillion-dollar industry that touches virtually every sector of the economy. Many of the world's largest global companies — household names you'd know, such as Apple Computer and Intel — were launched with money from private investors. And perhaps most relevant for you, many multibillion-dollar real estate empires relied exclusively on private money to get their businesses off the ground.

Will yours be the next multibillion-dollar real estate empire?

In the broad investment world, private money investments can take many forms; for example, startup loans from friends and family, angel investments, venture capital, mezzanine financing and factoring. But, the two most common forms of private investments for real estate are:

1. **Private Money Loans.** The private investor becomes "the bank," and receives a promissory note, and usually a mortgage or other security instrument on the property in exchange for earned interest; commonly used for financing smaller deals, such as single-family houses. You pay the note over a specified period of time; the loan structure might be interest-only or amortized. Interest might be repaid monthly, annually, or it may accrue in a lump sum to be paid with principal when the note is due.

2. **Private Money Equity Investments.** The investor becomes a part-owner of the property or project, committing funds in exchange for a share of the cash flows and profits from sale. This deal type is commonly used for larger projects, such as commercial and multi-family apartment deals, but can be used for smaller deals as well. Equity investments are unsecured, meaning the investor does not receive a mortgage or other security for their principal. Equity investors have the advantage of receiving cash flow and appreciation/gain on sale, which can present more attractive returns than receiving steady interest on a loan. Equity investors may also enjoy certain tax advantages over private money loans.

Which form of deals do private investors generally prefer? There's no one-size-fits-all answer. Different investors have different investment goals and financial objectives. Private money loans may offer investors a secured or collateralized investment and steady interest income — similar to, for example, a bond investment or Certificate of Deposit (CD). On the other hand, some investors prefer an equity investment, since it may offer higher profit potential and tax advantages.

Far too many real estate investors only see the lending side of the private money coin. They get caught up in only offering notes and mortgages to private investors without ever exploring the possibilities of bringing in equity investors.

For single-family house deals, such as a flips, a private mortgage loan usually makes the most sense — *usually*.

For bigger deals, however, such as apartment buildings or commercial properties, offering an equity investment to private investors becomes a great option. Moreover, if you're purchasing a large project with commercial financing, the commercial lender will almost always require that the down payment *not* be borrowed funds — so you'll have to bring in equity investors. When you finish this book, you'll have the wisdom to know when to use which type of private money deals. Part of the trick is matching the deal with the investor(s).

My preferred source of private money is equity investors. Most of the deals I do — even single-family houses — are easier and more profitable because I have equity investors. It may sound odd that someone would rather invest in a real estate deal with me for a piece of the profits instead of a fixed rate loan, but I'll show you later how it makes all the sense in the world.

The Private Money Difference
Often, novice real estate investors don't see the need for (and value of!) private money when they first launch their businesses. Most tend to first utilize other financing sources, such as mortgages or lines of credit. They struggle, maybe get a deal or two under their belts, and it suddenly dawns on them that life would be so much easier if they had private money.

I have a confession to make: I've just described myself — my first real estate deal. Every once in a while, the gruesome details of that deal come flooding back… I had to beg, borrow and steal to cobble together the down payment. I maxed out my credit, and — to add insult to injury — had to endure a difficult seller. (You can probably relate!) To this day, my overarching impression of that deal is *anxiety*. I went to bed every night (the closing date fast approaching), not knowing whether I'd even have the money to go to the closing table. Well, I did (barely); the deal closed, but by a narrow margin. And I resolved to *never* be in that position again. Later, when I got my first private money investor, the skies opened up. A huge burden had been lifted and I could, finally, confidently make offers secure in the knowledge that I could close every one of them. It was such a relief! And the beginning of my real success.

My goal is for you to never have to worry about whether you can come up with the cash to close. Through education, focus and concerted action, you'll have the freedom to choose the best deals, close 'em, cash 'em out and move on to the next opportunity.

Depending on your business goals, you may find many compelling reasons to use private money. Here are some examples of what private money can *immediately* do for your business:

- You can do more deals
- Pay "All Cash"
- Transcend the limitations of your personal resources and credit
- You can do larger deals
- Maximize your return on investment
- Grow your business

Now, let's look at each of these benefits in action…

Do More Deals

We all want to do more deals — of course we do! If getting that first $50,000 profit is fun, imagine how fun it will be to repeat it again and again. With private money, you can! By supplementing your existing financial resources with private money, you can do many more deals. For example, let's say you have $180,000 on hand and you want to buy an investment house for $140,000 that needs $30,000 worth of repairs. You can do the deal, but you won't be able to buy another property until you accumulate more savings, sell the house, or re-finance it.

If you qualify for a loan and successfully navigate through their maze of paperwork, banks and mortgage companies will typically finance only a portion of the purchase price — 80% or 90% — and *you* almost always have to fund the rehab. As you do more deals, your personal resources and financing sources could quickly be depleted. When you have private money, you can do as many deals as you want, with no limitations.

Fund "All-Cash" Deals

Often, paying "all cash" gets you the best deals. The ability to pay cash is a tremendous negotiating edge. When you've got the cash, the other party will deal with you more favorably; for starters, because your offer is not contingent on third party financing – meaning it's more of a sure thing to close. Paying all cash is especially advantageous when dealing with bank-owned or other distressed properties. Think about it: If a bank is asking $250,000 for a property they own and you offer $170,000, but you have to go get a mortgage, is the bank going to look as favorably upon your offer as they would if you could close quickly with all cash?

Having access to private money gives you the resources to pay cash and edge out your competition. The cash advantage alone has enabled me to do nearly *ten times* as many deals as I could have done with bank financing or hard money.

Transcend the Limitations of Your Personal Resources and Credit
Typically, banks will only loan you money on a certain number of properties, then they cut you off or sharply curtail the amount of money you can borrow. And banks rules change frequently, which is all the more reason to wean yourself from the habit of relying on them to finance you. For some reason, banks believe it is risky to finance investment properties (strange they don't see any risk in buying those convoluted mortgage securities…)

Also, banks want you to have some skin in the game, which means you have to come up with a cash down payment to close the deal. As your volume of bank-financed deals increases, the level of personal cash invested in your portfolio of properties increases. After only a few deals, it's amazing (and scary) how fast you can deplete your personal cash reserves.

Using private money helps preserve your own cash and credit. Preserving your own resources helps ensure that your business can withstand unexpected ups and downs in the future. In the midst of the most recent national real estate market changes, investors who were over-leveraged (had borrowed too much from banks) suffered the most. Having private money ensures that your business is financially sound, and you're not over-leveraged — you have backup cash reserves. Higher leverage translates to higher risk.

Do Larger Deals
Private money is critical for closing larger deals. When you start swimming in the deep end of the pool, you need to have some cash behind you. For example, if you want to invest in a 20-unit apartment building with a $1,000,000 purchase price and get commercial financing for 75% it, you need at least $250,000 for the down payment.

To buy an apartment deal like I just described, you'd also need to have sufficient cash in an operating reserve account to withstand a vacancy increase or unanticipated capital improvements. Unless you've got $250,000 lying around for all these type of deals you want to do, you're going to need private money.

Higher Return on Investment
If you supplement or replace your personal funds with private investor funds, your personal return on investment for each deal climbs higher and higher.

When you start doing deals with none of your own money, your return can reach infinity. Consider the following:

Let's say you buy a duplex using your own cash for down payment:

Figure 1.4

Duplex Purchase - Using Your Own Funds	
Purchase Price	$200,000
Loan amount (75% of purchase price)	$150,000
Cash Needed for Down Payment	$50,000
Annual Net Cash Flow	$8,000
Cash on Cash Return	16%

Now, look at your return on investment when you bring in a private investor:

Figure 1.5

Duplex Purchase - Using Private Money	
Purchase Price	$200,000
Loan amount (75% of purchase price)	$150,000
Private Money for Down Payment	$50,000
Private Investor Split	60%
Annual Net Cash Flow to Private Investor	$4,800
Cash on Cash Return - Private Investor	9.6%
Your Annual Net Cash Flow	$3,200
Your Return on Invesement	Infinite

See how your return on investment goes up in proportion to the amount of private money you bring in on the deal? In this example, you'd provide the private investor with a healthy 9.6% annual return (plus 60% of the sale profits when the duplex is sold), while giving yourself a nice *infinite* return on investment + $3,200 in your pocket each year + 40% of the sale profits. Your return is infinite because you are receiving cash flow with none of your own money invested.

Build a bigger business
Private money will help you build a strong, profitable business that will stand the test of time. Private money begets more private money, which leads to deals. Deals beget more deals. The buying power and momentum that comes with having access to private money is a big difference-maker.

A huge benefit of having the private money to do more, bigger and better deals is that you become the 'go-to' person. When someone else's deal falls through, *you* get the call to come in and scoop it up. If another buyer can't close, the deal goes to *you*. You can build a big (and lucrative) company by having a reputation as someone who can close.

I once got a frantic call from a real estate agent. One of his buyers was backing out of a deal just a few days before closing. If the deal didn't close, the agent's reputation would be tarnished with the listing bank. I was the first person on his call list. Several days later, my company closed on that property. A few days after that it sold for a healthy profit.

After the closing, I reflected on the deal, as I often do — looking for ways to improve for the future. At first, I was stumped. Why *did* I get the call? There were probably other investors that this agent could have called, so why did he choose me? Then it hit me: he called me because he knew *I had a reputation as a closer*. But, why was it a cinch for me to close? Because I had private money behind me. My entire real estate business has been built on this very simple concept. It works.

He who has the gold…
Ever heard the expression: "He who has the gold makes the rules…"? Well, nowhere is this truer than in real estate investing. If *location, location, location* is the first golden rule of real estate investment, then *cash, cash, cash* is the second rule.

Cash in the bank gives you confidence while providing you with an insurance policy against missed opportunities. You have the security of knowing that you can kick into gear and execute immediately when a great deal comes across your desk. You don't have to scramble from bank to bank, or produce mountains of last-minute loan application paperwork. You don't have to worry about future interest hikes on your credit lines. You don't have to risk your home to guarantee a loan. **Cash** enables you to play the game at a whole new level.

It's no secret that big players like Warren Buffet and Donald Trump always maintain reserves of 'dry powder' (cash in the bank) to ensure they always have the resources to pounce when golden opportunities come their way. For example, in 2008, when large global companies such as General Electric and Goldman Sachs were battered by the credit markets and the economic downturn, Warren Buffett had the cash on hand to supply the investment capital that Goldman Sachs, a venerable investment bank, so desperately needed. The result? Buffett earned a $3.1 billion return in less than a year.[i] And, even if you don't aspire to be the next Warren Buffett, you can still tack a few extra zeros onto your net worth using the same principles he uses.

Private Money Has Never Been More Necessary

In today's real estate market, *cash is king*. And there's never been a better time to focus on attracting private money than *now*. You won't find many bank asset managers (tasked with unloading foreclosed real estate in million dollar chunks) who are willing to entertain offers contingent on financing! Each day that you delay getting private money, you're missing a *huge* opportunity to capitalize on the "all you can eat" buffet of bargain real estate. No matter what technique you use for acquiring or selling properties, private money will be the multi-million dollar difference for you.

First Deal Syndrome

Now, if you haven't closed your first real estate deal yet, you're probably thinking that you've got no chance of attracting private money. Not true! You can absolutely attract private money, *even if you've never done a deal before.*

How? You must demonstrate to investors that the deal will be successful — their money is safe in your hands. (We'll come back to this in a minute. Everyone is nervous about their first private money deal. No matter how focused, competent, or prepared you are, that first deal can be fraught with unexpected perils. My first six-figure private money deal was nerve-wracking.

It was for $110,000 private money loan. I'd been working this potential investor for weeks and weeks, and finally, he agreed to sit down with me over coffee to discuss the details. I had several options that I could offer him. I had done my due diligence — I was *prepared*. Or so I thought.

The meeting started off on the right foot. We exchanged pleasantries for a few minutes. We sipped coffee, chatted about our respective businesses, the market — so far, so good. Then things began to go horribly awry…

For the next ten minutes, my potential new investor proceeded to regale me with a horror story… He'd just gotten burned on a private money deal with another real estate investor and was currently in foreclosure on the property! He was not at all happy about this private lending experience.

I was mortified — speechless, by the time he finished this tale of woe. How was I supposed to respond to this? What could I possibly say to turn him around? My heart was pounding and my throat felt parched. Beads of sweat popped up on my forehead. The silence was deafening. I could hear the whisper of the ventilation system, or maybe it was the cold hiss of air leaking out of my deal, my little balloon of hope now completely deflated. What happened next was as an even bigger shock.

This investor looked me in the eye and said: "You seem very trustworthy and I'm going to invest with you. If things go well, I have some additional money that I'd like to invest."

What?! Did he just say he was going to invest money with me? I sat there for a few seconds, dumbfounded. I had just gotten a loan commitment and didn't even have to ask for it! It was like a dream!

You may be asking: how did this deal go through in spite of the private lender's bad experience?

I simply trusted my system and techniques. I relied on proven private money attraction principles. That's what closed the deal for me. And that system is what you will find within the pages of this book.

The first secret you must know about getting private money is this: *Investors bet on the jockey, not the horse.* Your goal is to become the jockey they bet on.

Chapter 2

Why Should They Invest With You?

How do people choose investments? What drives private money investing? Why would someone investment money with you?

There are five key private money drivers:
- Higher returns
- Diversification
- Easier to Understand Investments
- Personal Interests
- *You*

Higher Returns

Many private investors will place funds with you because you are offering them higher returns than they can realize from other investments. So, *why* will your deals yield higher returns? Because, by finding undervalued properties and turning them into profits, you are literally creating wealth! When you create tremendous amounts of value, your investors are rewarded by participating in this value creation.

The higher returns you offer your investors will make a huge difference for them. Let's say you're offering your investor a 12% return on a private money note. If you compare the return you're offering against the stock market (which historically averages returns of roughly 10% per year) over a period of 20 years, you'd get the following result:

Figure 2.1

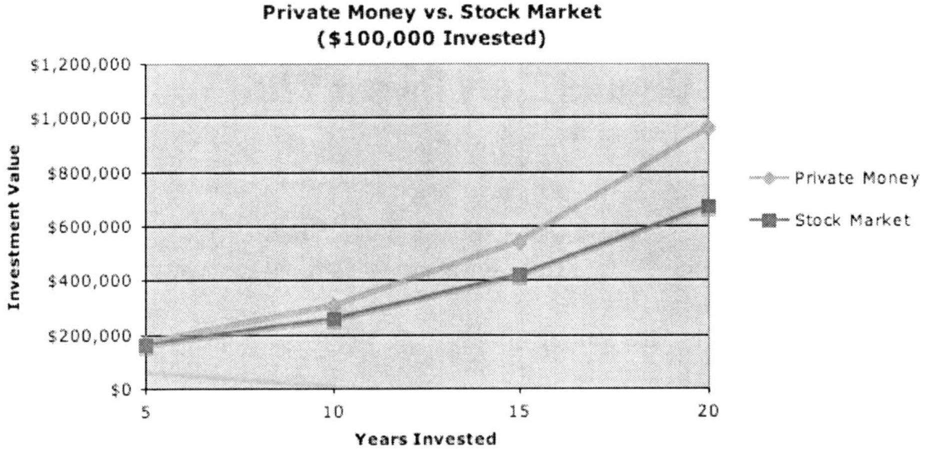

**Private Money vs. Stock Market
($100,000 Invested)**

The hard numbers in figure 2.1 show how private investors benefit from investing with you at a 12% rate of return versus the stock market yielding its long-term average return of 10% per year. Even after just five years invested, the private investor would be $15,583 ahead of the stock market. Over a period of 20 years, the difference of just a few percentage points per year compounded is worth hundreds of thousands of dollars!

Diversification

Many private money investors like to diversify their investment portfolios, instead of "putting all their eggs in one basket," such as having all their retirement funds tied up in the stock market. The theory behind diversification is, by spreading investment capital across multiple asset classes, the likelihood of big losses to the *total* portfolio is unlikely. The financial services industry — through heavy marketing and sales pitches delivered by financial planners and stockbrokers — tends to influence investor thinking by emphasizing diversification as a strategy for avoiding big financial losses.

Some investors may view private money investing as diversification from the stock market, bond market, mutual funds, or as diversification from other assets they may hold, such as commodities. In a way, our 'friends' in the financial services industry have done us a big favor by telling investors that they should diversify. Investing with you in real estate is a great way to accomplish this objective.

Many private investors make the mistake of thinking they can achieve diversification in their investments through mutual funds or similar vehicles alone. This is an erroneous assumption. Here's a sample portfolio of a typical private money investor (prior to investing with you):

Figure 2.2

**Typical Investor Portfolio
No Private Money Investment**

Other 20%
CDs 10%
Cash 15%
Mutual Funds 55%

A private investor will actually achieve true diversification by investing in your real estate deal, because they are then invested in a completely *different asset class*.

Here's a sample portfolio for the same investor once they make an investment with you:

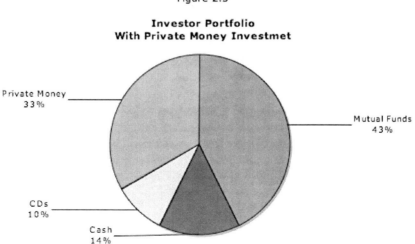

Figure 2.3

**Investor Portfolio
With Private Money Investmet**

Private Money 33%
CDs 10%
Cash 14%
Mutual Funds 43%

You can see that the investor's portfolio is better balanced than it was before. And this example is a great selling point that you can use to demonstrate to private investors why it makes sense to invest with you.

Easier-to-Understand Investment

People invest in what they *understand*. If it comes down to investing in something they don't understand or hiding the money under the mattress, the mattress wins out. Many people invest in private money deals because it's an investment they understand. Private investors are comfortable with real estate because it is a tangible investment – something they can see, touch and feel. It's not mysterious, like sending a check off into the wild blue yonder for a confusing, complex financial instrument managed by a big company that changes names every two months.

A private mortgage investment, for example, is a process investors have likely experienced when purchasing their own home. This may be a more comfortable investment than a mutual fund, stock or bond. It's also worth mentioning that many people distrust Wall Street and the financial establishment, especially considering their nest-egg value may whipsaw up and down with no rhyme or reason. The Wall Street bank bailouts have bred additional distrust among many investors, making private money investment in real estate all the more attractive.

Personal Interest.

Some people are attracted to private money investing because they have an interest, a special knowledge, passion or affinity for the specific industry or market niche they're investing in. For example, some private money investors in real estate are retired real estate agents, brokers or former real estate attorneys.

Many wealthy investors have an enthusiasm for investing in entrepreneurial ventures that are dedicated to creating good jobs, building communities, and building a more productive society to ensure that future generations will enjoy a higher standard of living.

$$$$ **Resource** $$$$

Find out more about what makes Private Investors tick.
Sign up for the free 10 week email course at
www.TheBookonPrivateMoney.com.
We cover the private investor psyche in-depth in Lesson #4

$$$$$$

Why You?

It's important to never lose sight of the private investor's real question. The question is not *Why should I invest in this deal?* The real question is *Why should I invest with YOU?*

If somebody tells you that all private investors care about are "the numbers" or the "return on investment," don't believe them. Nothing could be further from the truth. Private investors, no matter what their net worth, are not financial robots. They're human, just like the rest of us. And like the rest of us, they face their own personal and professional challenges, they have good days and bad days, and they forge emotional connections with some people, but not others. Trust, of course, is required for that emotional connection.

Rarely will you meet an investor who's purely focused on the financial aspects of the deal at the beginning of your relationship. In the beginning, they're focused on *you. Do I like you? Do I trust you? Do I want to do business with you?* Whether consciously or unconsciously, the prospect who's pondering whether or not to invest in your deal is essentially asking the question: *Why choose this partner?*

Why do investors choose one partner over another? More often than not, the reason is *trust*. Delivering on your promises is how you build trust. And trust is that intangible, intuitive silent partner that we rely on to help us make investment decisions. In the absence of a more compelling reason, we'll buy what we trust. Meet and beat your investor's expectations the first time, the second time, every time, and you'll forge an emotional bond that can last a lifetime.

When it comes to private money, here's what it really comes down to:

You — can the investor trust *you*?
You — does the investor believe that *you* can deliver what you promise?
The deal — does the investment make sense, in general?
The deal — does the investment make sense for the investor?
Timing — is the timing right?

You can never lose sight of the fact that your investor always has a choice, even if your deal has no competition. They can choose to invest in something else. They can choose to do nothing. They always have a choice.

That choice could be you.

Next, we'll work on *YOU*...

PART II

Private Money Attraction Principles

Ben Franklin, widely acknowledged as one of the wisest and wealthiest individuals of his time, once said: "An investment in knowledge always pays the best interest."ii He said this over 230 years ago, but truer words were never spoken. Investing in yourself and your business will pay huge dividends.

What has enabled me to generate seven figure private money sums? In a nutshell:

1. I focused on private money.
2. I set private money goals.
3. I committed myself to achieving them.

If you aspired to be an architect, you'd first have to learn the fundamental principles of building design. If you aspired to be an auto mechanic, you'd have to learn the fundamental principles of how cars work. When Orville and Wilbur Wright were getting their first plane off the ground, they utilized fundamental principles of physics and aerodynamics. All worthy endeavors in life are governed by fundamental principles — laws that must be followed to ensure a successful result.

To get private money, there are fundamental principles that must be followed. The next few chapters will reveal my Private Money Attraction Principles. They form the heart and soul of my entire private money approach. Over the next five chapters, we'll take an in-depth look at each principle.

When you use these principles to guide your actions, you will attract private money. If you choose to ignore these principles, any private money success you have will be sporadic, fleeting, or unpredictable. I can promise you this: Getting as much private money as you need is much easier when you put these principles to work on a daily basis.

Chapter 3

Private Money Attraction Principle #1

Focus

We live in a fast-paced, ever-changing world. We live busier, more competitive lives than our ancestors did, thanks to an increasingly global economic environment. Modern life requires us to be ambidextrous jugglers. The To-Do lists seem to grow longer and longer, don't they? Every day, we find ourselves juggling work, family, and community obligations, and — let's face it — not always as well as we'd like. Often, it's hard to keep all the balls in the air on a daily basis.

Every day, all day long, we're bombarded with information — advertising messages, emails, sales pitches, prospectuses, and the particulars of deals, deals, deals — lots of shiny objects competing for our attention and distracting us from our true purpose. Filtering out what is not helping you achieve your goals requires a single-minded dedication to purpose — *focus*.

Are you ready to propel your business to the next level? Getting private money is the key to getting there, whether your goal is to go from flipping one house per year to one house per month, or to expand a portfolio of 3 rental houses to 30, or 4 units under management to 400. And the way to get private money (in short order) is to develop a *private money focus*: Make attracting private investors a core *focus* of your business.

Your goal is to fill your pipeline with private investors who are just begging to do deals with you. No matter what system you use to buy, sell or manage your properties, private money is the key to success — for any real estate investing business. And getting private money is much easier than you think.

Far too many real estate investors spend *zero time* attracting private money, and then wonder why private investors aren't banging down their door. Eventually private investors will simply come to you, as if by magic. But in the beginning, *you'll need to apply a little elbow grease*. If you simply allocate a few hours each week to focusing on attracting private money, you may be shocked at how much money you'll be able to generate, and how quickly. You'll never have to worry about banks or mortgage brokers again.

Napoleon Hill discusses the concept of focus in his work *The Laws of Success*, the precursor to his timeless classic *Think and Grow Rich*. Hill determined the laws of success by chronicling the greatest businessmen of his time (men such as: Andrew Carnegie, John D. Rockefeller, and Charles Schwab). He describes "a definite chief aim," where "eliminating aimlessness and wasted effort" [iii] are key drivers of success. Focus is a success principle that always works, but one that many real estate investors ignore. Devoting even small, incremental blocks of time and focus to attracting private money will yield results.

In one of my favorite books, *The Seven Habits of Highly Effective People*, Steven Covey points out that ultra successful people "begin with the end in mind." (Habit #2).[iv] I love this concept, and have personally found it to be incredibly powerful. It's a rule to live by, and it's easy to do…

Start by envisioning the result of getting private money. Envision what you will do with it. Set your target. Picture your offers getting considered first. Picture yourself tearing up those dreaded mortgage applications. Now… picture your business bank account balance at $100,000, $500,000, $1,500,000… just waiting for a deal to pull the trigger on. This is your end goal. Thousands and thousands of dollars in cash flowing to you each month, big chunks of 5-figure profits, year-in and year-out. This exercise in focus will help you *see* each daily action step you take as part of your overall plan for private money within the framework of your business.

Let me tell you about a day that marked a turning point in my business…

When I first began setting private money goals, I wrote them on a piece of paper and tacked them to the bulletin board behind my computer — where I couldn't possibly miss seeing them every day. These goals were real, tangible, and actionable, but day after day they just stared back at me… I had no idea where to start.

$$$$ **Resource** $$$$

Start off on the right foot by setting private money goals.
Sign up for the free 10 week email course at
www.TheBookonPrivateMoney.com.

$$$$$$

Each day, a deal would come and go across my desk, a deal that I would have made a tidy profit on, if only I had enough cash to close — if only I had private money. One day, I remembered a quote my father once shared with me when I was a teenager. At the time, I was frustrated because I didn't make the starting lineup on my high school basketball team. "You miss a hundred percent of the shots you don't take…" he told me. Well, no one likes a ball hog, but on the other hand, I was never going to be a starter if I didn't shoot more — and prove myself to the coaches. I took his advice to heart, and my playing time increased dramatically.

Flash forward to my private money goals staring at me from the wall…

I realized that if I didn't start taking shots, actively talking to — and proposing deals to — investors, if I didn't take at least one step each day toward finding and getting private money investors, those goals would just keep staring at me, unfulfilled. I started taking focused, purposeful action that day, in earnest. And my efforts paid big dividends. Soon, people were asking *me* if they could invest with *me*. That's a great position to be in. It's my hope that you will come to experience that same sense of security and opportunity.

If you're serious about getting private investors, spend some time every day focusing on private money, *envisioning* your results.

Get Focused

How do you get focused on private money? First, realize that if you have real estate goals, *by default,* you have private money goals. It's powerfully effective. Next, chart it on paper. I broke down my deals and profits, and the private money sum I needed to get there. Here's what it looked like:

Figure 3.1

Private Money Targeting - Single Family Houses	
Annual Profit Goal	$150,000
Profit per Deal	$30,000
Deals per Year Needed	5
Average Deal Cost	$100,000
Holding Time	3 months
Private Money Needed	**$200,000**

Setting targets like this was how I was able to set achievable private money goals for myself. I broke it down into discrete and actionable steps. In fact, I could have broken the private money amount needed into smaller increments (which I still often do), such as: 4 investors at $50,000 each or 8 investors at $25,000 each.

My private money goals were based on my initial business strategy, which was flipping single-family houses. Suppose your goal was to acquire apartment buildings for cash flow; you might break down your private money goals like this:

Figure 3.2

Private Money Targeting - Apartment Buildings	
Annual Profit Goal	$100,000
Annual Net Cash Flow per Building	$25,000
Buildings Needed	4
Average Building Cost	$500,000
Equity Needed Per Building	$125,000
Private Money Needed	**$500,000**

These examples are simple for a reason: Your private money goals need to be as simple and concrete as possible. If you start throwing all kinds of variables into the mix, you'll get distracted. Set a nice, round target number and pursue it aggressively.

Grab a pencil and paper and determine your private money goals, using these examples as guidelines. Don't be afraid to be aggressive — just make sure you're specific. Staying focused on private money every day will yield amazing results.

Private Money is a Function of Time Allocation

Focusing on private money is likely to mean allocating your time differently. We all have 24 hours in a day, but some people are more effective with how they use those 24 hours than others. You must devote an appropriate portion of your time to marketing your business for private money, as well as finding and cultivating relationships with private investors.

Every time a real estate investor tells me that they don't have any private investors, my immediate reaction is to ask them how much time they're spending on getting private investors. In fact, over the years, I've observed other real estate investors extensively, and have found that the average real estate investor's time allocation works out like this:

Figure 3.3

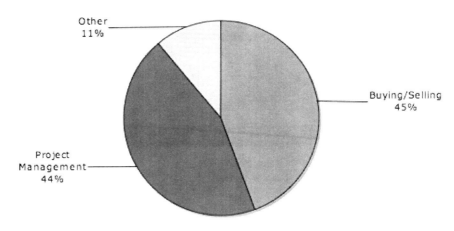

The bulk of the average real estate investor's time (45%) is spent on acquiring and selling properties, and the remainder spent on project management (44%) and other activities, such as administration and general business management (11%).

Contrast the time allocation of the average real estate investor to that of a successful investor that works with large sums of private money:

Figure 3.4

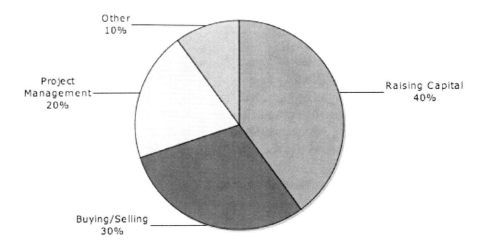

The majority of the successful investor's time (40%) is spent on marketing and cultivating relationships with private investors. Acquiring and selling properties takes approximately 30% of their time, and the remainder is split between project management (20%) and other activities (10%).

It should come as no surprise that focus leads to better time allocation, and better time allocation leads directly to the desired result: private money. You can't spend zero time acquiring investors and then wonder why nobody is beating down your door to fund your deals. Look at any successful person — athlete, entertainer or business executive — and you'll find that the results they achieve are directly related to the amount of time they invest in <u>themselves.</u>

Would Michael Jordan have been the best basketball player of his era if he didn't focus and allocate his time toward that goal? No. Would Oprah Winfrey be a media mogul without productively using her time? No. Take a page from the ultra-successful: FOCUS.

You must make private money a focus in your business.

Chapter 4

Private Money Attraction Principle #2:

Integrity

On a beautiful autumn day in Michigan, I was speaking to a room full of ambitious real estate investors. The group was as lively a crowd as I had ever spoken to, but one man in particular kept insistently raising his hand and asking questions. Normally this would have been disruptive, but this man was different.

He was not American and spoke in broken English. At a critical juncture in my discussion of integrity (which is more effective when delivered in a continuous flow), he interrupted me again, waving frantically to get my attention. Not wanting to break momentum, I tried to press on, hoping he'd get the message and hold his questions until the designated Q&A period. No such luck. Finally, I surrendered.

"Did you have a question?" I asked him.

"Yes," he said.

"Okay, shoot…" I replied

What he said next was so profound that I ended up *thanking* him for his question. This man asked: "Adam, you mention integrity…I find this mentioned so often, but it is one of the most confusing words in the English language. Can you please define this for me?" The attention of everyone in the room, heretofore focused on this man, now swiveled to me.

Indeed, what *is* integrity? What a fascinating and complex question. Integrity, naturally, requires adhering to a moral or ethical code. Lately, it's gotten harder to find stellar examples of integrity in our industry. In fact, it seems that integrity has been all but extinguished from the business world at large. Take your pick: Enron, Bernie Madoff, the Wall Street meltdown — each symbolizes massive and very public breaches of integrity in business. Integrity seems to have been surgically removed from the curriculum of business schools. Even in popular culture, movies like *Wall Street* and *Capitalism: A Love Story*, indict business ethics on a massive scale.

Is it any wonder that the overwhelming majority of us distrust Wall Street, and the corporate world in general? Skepticism is rampant, all the more reason for you to do business with integrity. You may find that some of your new private investors are actually looking for a reason to *distrust* you.

I once heard a definition of integrity that has served me well: *Integrity is doing what's right when nobody else is looking*. I love this definition of integrity. It simply has to be true. When you do what's right — if you *always* do what's right, even if nobody is looking, you have integrity. In the real estate business, we're often faced with temptations and choices that can lead to taking shortcuts. That escrow overage check from the title company that's $25 too much. Or that crack in a house's foundation that can easily be concealed from a buyer's eyes.

Life is a summation of the choices we make each day. Your business and your reputation is the totality of the choices you make every day. From the little things to the major aspects of a real estate transaction.

Perhaps you're wondering what all this has to do with getting private money, but I promise you: *It has everything to do with it*. I can't overemphasize this. You are only as valuable to your investors as your reputation, and your reputation will most certainly be built from your acts of integrity… or the lack of them. Word gets around. Real estate may be a multinational, multitrillion-dollar industry, but word gets around.

If you don't conduct business with integrity, you can forget about attracting private money. If you have no integrity, private investors won't trust you. If they don't trust you, they won't invest money with you. Think about it…would you invest your money with someone whose integrity was questionable? Not likely.

Same goes for your private investors. It breaks down like this: integrity means private money *attraction*. No integrity is a private money repellant.

Pretty simple, right?

In today's business climate, integrity is actually a competitive edge! Considering the recent scandals in the financial industry, real estate investors with integrity are a breath of fresh air to private investors. Integrity begins with honesty. Fair deals. Full disclosure. You will always face the temptation to do whatever it takes to get the deal done. I do believe in pulling out all the stops and removing all the obstacles that might discourage investors from placing their funds with you, but do *not* lie, embellish or omit. And you must deliver on your promises.

Never lie to private investors about your background, accomplishments or past performance. You can concentrate on your more positive attributes in your presentation, but you cannot omit critical information or give an investor false or misleading information. With all the B.S. going out there in the world today, any investor worth having will appreciate your integrity. Always have your private investors' best interests at heart. Remember, you are using someone else's money, and it's your responsibility to be a good steward of that money.

Does 'Win-Win' Still Exist?
A plethora of business books have been published over the last 25 years, and those books have pretty much beaten the concept of "Win-Win" to death. We've become rather cavalier about that phrase; however, 'win-win' is still valid. It still works. It still builds businesses. The best way to make the private money attraction principle of integrity work for you is to make sure that your deals are fundamentally sound and that you're confident that you can fully execute the details. This doesn't mean that all risks are removed or that you're guaranteeing a profit every time. But it does mean that you're not putting your investors in deals that you don't believe in, or worse, that you *know* will result in financial loss for them. Because there are so many unscrupulous investments out there, you must work that much harder to stand apart.

Remember the Biblical parable of the talents? Before going away on a long journey, a master entrusted his three servants with his property, each according to his ability. To one, he gave 5 talents; to the second, he gave 2 talents; to the third, he gave 1 talent. A talent was a valuable precious metal, equal to more than 15 years' wages of a laborer.

When the master returned, he was eager to see what each servant had done with the talents he had been given. The first servant had turned the 5 talents into 10. The second servant had turned his 2 talents into 4. The master was pleased, and told each of them. "Well done, good and faithful servant. You have been faithful over a little, so I will set you over much."

The third servant had done nothing with his 1 talent; he buried it in the ground. He told his master: "Master, I knew you to be a hard man, reaping what you did not sow, so, I was afraid."

"You wicked and slothful servant!" exclaimed the master. "You ought to have invested my money with the bankers, and at my coming I should have received what was mine with interest." And he took the talent and gave it to the first servant who had 10 talents, telling the third servant: "To those who have, more will be given, and he will have abundance. But from him who has not, even what he has will be taken away."v

Powerful lesson, isn't it? This parable teaches us that we must use wisely the "talents" we are given. You must be a good steward of the private money you accept. One fundamental and timeless principle of money is that if you use it wisely, more will come your way.

Using a private investor's money doesn't feel the same as using your own money, or even using bank money. Someone is trusting you with their hard earned investment dollars. Don't be nervous about it. Just make sure that you never lose sight of the integrity money attraction principle.

Make sure that your interests are aligned with those of your investors. Every deal you do with private money should yield rewards for you *and* your investors. Having integrity doesn't mean that you're required to sacrifice an extraordinary or disproportionate percentage of profits. But having integrity does mean that you don't design deals that allow you to gain while your investor loses.

Let me give you an example...

You purchase an investment property for $100,000. You estimate its after-repair value to be $170,000. You get $140,000 in private money for this property for the purposes of purchase and rehab. Upon closer inspection, you realize that the property will need just $15,000 for the rehab. You pocket that extra chunk of private money ($140K – $115K = $25K) - without telling your investor where *all* the money is going.

What's wrong with this picture? Well, ask yourself how you would feel if *you* were the private investor and your real estate investor skimmed a nice profit off the top, before the deal even sells *and* you had no idea that the unneeded rehab money was going into the real estate investor's pocket? The real estate investor has already made a nice profit by taking a big piece of the equity up front, so they may have less incentive to move the property quickly.

Always set up your private money deals so that mutual gain is assured — start to finish. This is 'win-win'. When your interests and motives don't align with your investor's, you can quickly find yourself in a sticky situation.

Warren Buffett, arguably one of the world's greatest investors, is fond of saying that if your behavior would embarrass you, should it end up on the front page of tomorrow's paper, then you shouldn't do it.[vi] He's right. If you find your integrity wavering in the face of temptation, ask yourself whether your choice would embarrass you, if everyone was looking. If the answer is Yes, don't do it.

Private money is attracted to those who do business with integrity. Integrity always shines through, and private investors are more than happy to place money with those who have it. I guarantee it.

Chapter 5

Private Money Attraction Principle #3:

Transparency

trans·par·ent: *Capable of transmitting light so that objects or images can be seen as if there were no intervening material; free from guile; candid or open.*

Transparency goes hand in hand with integrity, and it's a pivotal private money attraction principle. If you have integrity, you'll do business with transparency.

Transparency, in private money investing, means that your private investors always know how you're using their money and that you're giving them the whole story. Transparency must exist on all levels with your investors — even with little things, like signing the right mortgage paperwork and making proper cash distributions. The more transparent you are with your private investors, the more respect you will garner.

Transparency is the one private money attraction principle that, if violated, can have the most damaging effects on your reputation, and your ability to do business in the future. If you doubt this, take a quick glance at the business news headlines. These days, it's easy to mistake the business section for the crime section…

"Burned! How Greedy Execs and Clueless Accountants Left Enron Bankrupt and the Little Guy in the Lurch."[vii]

" WorldCom scandal one of many: It may be involved in the biggest accounting debacle ever, but financial scandals are nothing new.."[viii]

Everywhere we turn, we hear tales of backroom deals cloaked in subterfuge, companies that are violating anti-trust laws, financial officers cooking the books. The masterminds behind these schemes deliberately shrouded their actions in secrecy, believing they'd never get caught. But they did. Next thing you know, they're doing the perp walk, but not before they've bilked investors out of their life savings and destroyed the livelihoods of loyal employees who had no idea that their bosses were no better than street thugs.

Scary headlines make investors squeamish about investing their hard earned money. This is why it's so important to maintain transparency with your private investors. When people can't see where their money's going, they'll pull back, pull out, or never buy in to begin with — it's as simple as that.

Your investors should know what their money is up to at all times. It's important to provide some form of statement or update to keep investors informed about what their money is doing and how the deal is performing. Be careful not to commingle funds between different investors for different projects, or use an investor's funds for purposes other than what they agreed to.

For instance, let's say you have a private lender who invests $150,000 with you to purchase and rehab a single-family house. If you use some of those funds for your other business operations, you're already losing transparency, unless the investor has explicitly approved this use of their funds. You must always obtain the investor's permission if you intend to allocate funds for any purpose other than the purpose he or she agreed to.

---————$$$$ Resource $$$$————---
Start off on the right foot by setting private money goals.
Sign up for the free 10 week email course at
www.TheBookonPrivateMoney.com.
We cover proper deal structuring in Lessons #3 and #10.
———————$$$$$$———————

It's tempting for a real estate investor to rationalize that, because the private investor has a mortgage or other security, the funds can be used for any business purpose. This mode of thinking will ultimately *repel* private money — you can count on it. Large financial services companies must disclose to their investors how the investors' funds are being allocated, right?

Think about it...

Suppose you write a check to your financial planner with instructions to invest the full amount in a stock mutual fund. But the financial planner invests 75% of the money in that stock fund and 25% in a bond fund. You'd be outraged that your financial planner breached your agreement by arbitrarily investing 25% of your money in bonds. Well, the same holds true for your real estate deals. Your private investors should know how their money is being used.

Now, suppose you have a private mortgage lender (as in the above example). What should you do if you need working capital or other funds to operate your business? You can simply provide the investor with a detailed funding allocation before the deal closes. If you show your investors what needs to be done and how their funds will be allocated, everything is above-board — you've made full disclosure.

When you are first proposing a deal, you may fear how the investor will react if you tell them that part of their investment will need to fund some of the other operations associated with the deal. A lot of real estate investors worry about this, but I've never had any problems. Explain to the investor why it makes sense to allocate some funds to working capital or a "buffer" fund. Explain *why* this allocation ensures the project's success.

One of the biggest reasons transparency is such a critical private money attraction principle is that there is so little of it elsewhere in the world. It is a breath of fresh air whereas most investment offers are wrapped in convoluted jargon and confusing fees. Bernie Madoff, who was the author of the biggest single financial swindle in history, was said to have developed a "black box" investment model[ix], a model so complex that nobody but him could understand it. Setting aside the ethical ramifications of transparency for a moment, it is simply a timeless and fundamental principle of business that if you differentiate yourself from everyone else, you'll achieve greater success.

You'll always be more successful if you stand apart from the pack — from your marketing materials to your fundamental way of doing business with transparency and integrity. As the old saying goes, drink upstream from the herd.

It's important to be able to tell investors — and mean it — that you do business the WYSIWYG Way. "What You See Is What You Get."

Chapter 6

Private Money Attraction Principle #4:

Confidence

As you embark upon your quest to bring private money into your business, you should begin to feel a powerful and pervasive sense of optimism. Along with this sense of optimism should be a sense of confidence. Just think: You're that much closer to waving good bye to banks and mortgage brokers, forever.

People will invest in what (and who) they like, what (and who) they understand and what (and who) they believe in. They're investing in *you*. They must like you, understand the investment, and believe in you.

The investor's confidence in your personal trustworthiness and in your ability to get the job done is that intangible factor that will continue to generate a steady stream of private investors throughout your career. Confidence can be the difference in getting an investor to invest $500,000 or $5,000,000. Many real estate entrepreneurs have all the other tools, but they lack confidence in themselves — thus can't inspire an investor's confidence. They lose out.

Let's clear up a few things about confidence…

Number one, you don't have to become a completely different person — you just have to be a confident *you*. You don't have to become a narcissistic jerk (in fact, you'd better *not*). You don't need to be arrogant or cocky. But you do need a healthy dose of confidence in the company you've built, in your project, and in your ability to provide investors a good return on their investment. This means you must be able to communicate your knowledge and enthusiasm to your investors so that they never have one shred of doubt that you can get the job done.

In my early days of drumming up private money, I always told myself this: "If the investor says no, I want them to say no for any reason other than a lack of faith in me." As I continued to refine my system and techniques of generating a consistent private money flow, I began to hear 'no' less and less.

Communicating your enthusiasm for the deal and for your business is a critical part of building confidence with your investors. Would you invest with someone who seems to have no personal enthusiasm for what they are asking you to buy?

Fortune Favors the Bold

You must be bold — yes, *bold* — each time you talk to an investor. Now, bold doesn't mean pushy or bossy or loud or obnoxious. You don't need to intimidate your investors (it won't work, anyway). No one likes being intimidated or bullied. Intimidation is not the best strategy for convincing someone to invest money with you.

The brand of boldness that works with private investors is simply about being brave, direct and clear about what you want — *unwavering*. Never waver or waffle. Waffling undermines an investor's confidence in you. If you're proposing a 10% private mortgage investment to a private lender, don't be wishy-washy about it. Be direct. Come right out and tell them you're proposing a 10% return. This will show the investor you're confident and that you know what you want. You've got a goal, and you're setting out to achieve it. They're working with you to achieve that end.

Put another way, if you waffle with the investor, they'll assume that you'll be a pushover when dealing with brokers, contractors or other investors on deals that involve *their* money. They're expecting you to protect and defend every penny of their return.

Remember, you're making a proposal to the investor. Proposals done with confidence always land better. Which of these marriage proposals do you think would be more effective: *"Will you marry me?"* or... *"Ah...I was kind of thinking that, well...you and I get along well and ah...well, if you're open to it, I thought that...maybe we could talk about getting married..."*

The first one has worked well for centuries — it's simple, direct, decisive, bold and underpinned by conviction. The second one will either evoke pity or get you laughed at (and neither result is good), but it doesn't have much hope of provoking an enthusiastic "Yes."

In your quest for private money, you're going for the enthusiastic "Yes." And confidence is how you get there.

Chapter 7

Private Money Attraction Principle #5:

Preparation

As the old saying goes, luck happens when preparation meets opportunity. You won't attract private money if you're unprepared. It's a good business practice to be as prepared as possible for any situation — especially for bringing investment capital into your business.

What exactly does 'being prepared' mean? Working through every last detail before you ever meet with an investor, saying the right words when you first meet an investor, streamlining the process so that investing with you is easy…and more (all of which we'll cover in upcoming chapters).

I won't pull any punches here: 99% of real estate investors are completely unprepared for attracting private money. Ninety-nine percent. *You* can be in that other 1 percent.

Most real estate investors don't have a plan for what to do in order to get the investment commitment, let alone what to do next if they should somehow accidentally manage to get a $250,000 check from a private investor. Often, being prepared is the difference between getting the check and walking away empty-handed. Prepare yourself and your business for private money, as if the money were a welcome houseguest you were happy to accommodate.

Preparation Means Removing Barriers

Imagine that you're an air traffic controller — air traffic controllers must always be in a state of preparedness. When you're preparing for a plane to land, you make must sure there are no other planes in the flight path and no vehicles or other objects on the runway where the plane will land. You must make sure that emergency response crews are standing by in case anything goes wrong with the landing. In order for the plane to land safely, you must remove all *obstacles and barriers*.

The same principle applies to getting private money. In order to land your deal safely, you must be prepared. And your preparation must include a plan for answering objections — removing obstacles from the runway.

Start by evaluating your business from the standpoint of your private investor. What questions or potential issues would a private investor see with placing funds with you? What can you do to remove those barriers and overcome those objections before they even materialize?

As real estate investors, we're often so excited about our businesses and so focused on success that we operate with blinders on. We only see what's right in front of us instead of what's going on around us. Be aware of what's going on in other businesses and industries, so you can prepare your business for any unexpected changes. The multitude of economic factors that impact the real estate industry are many, but knowing a few key ones (interest rates or existing home sales and trends) can help you better prepare your business for long term success.

When you prepare your business for the future, even by giving it some basic thought, your private investors will pick up on this and will be impressed by it. A strong and profitable real estate investing business that continually generates fantastic profits results from good preparation.

Preparation means *expectation*
Expectation means that you are anticipating an imminent result or action. If the weather forecaster is predicting rain, you prepare by packing your umbrella — you're expecting rain. Even if it doesn't rain, you were prepared. Better safe than sorry. If you prepare for getting private money, your mind is in expectation mode.

When you prepare, you create an expectation of tangible results. And interestingly, the subconscious mind has a hard time discerning the difference between vivid imagery and reality. Let me tell you about a visualization experiment that was conducted by Australian psychologist Alan Richardson. Writer Keith Randolph recounted this fantastic research as follows:

> "The goal of the experiment was to test the impact of visualization in athletic activities. Richardson chose three groups of students at random. None had ever practiced visualization. The first group practiced free throws every day for twentieth days. The second made free throws on the first day and the twentieth day, as did the third group. But members of

the third group spent 20 minutes every day visualizing free throws. If they "missed," they "practiced" getting the next shot right.

On the twentieth day Richardson measured the percentage of improvement in each group. The group that practiced daily improved 24 percent. The second group, unsurprisingly, improved not at all. The third group, which had physically practiced no more than the second, did twenty-three percent better—almost as well as the first group!

In his paper on the experiment, published in Research Quarterly, Richardson wrote that the most effective visualization occurs when the visualizer feels and sees what he is doing. In other words, the visualizers in the basketball experiment "felt" the ball in their hands and "heard" it bounce, in addition to "seeing" it go through the hoop."[x]

The moral of the story? When you repeatedly visualize a certain result, the result is more likely to become reality. When you continue to *expect* a certain result, your brain begins to hard-wire your thoughts and behaviors for achieving that result. The basketball players who visualized success achieved it. So can you.

As you begin to open up relationships with private investors and word starts to gets out about your business (in a good way), it will become increasingly important that you are ready for every handshake and every meeting. Don't let opportunities pass you by. When you're prepared, you can be confident in knowing you won't miss any six-figure private money checks.

PART III

How to Get Private Investors

If private money is the Holy Grail of real estate investing, *marketing* for private money is the map to the Holy Grail. The one question people ask me more than any other is: *"Where do I find private investors?" Where?* is the burning question — for every real estate investor, without fail.

The answer? Well, if you're hoping for a silver bullet, I'm about to disappoint you. There is no silver bullet. There is no single guaranteed source of private money. (If there were, everyone who wanted it would have it.) And, this is good news: there are *many* sources waiting to be tapped.

Finding and bringing investors into your business is a little like big game hunting. You must hunt where the big game is and your aim must be sure. Contrary to what many novice real estate investors believe, private investors are not some rare and exotic species. You don't have to have a special permit to hunt them. You don't have to know a secret handshake to be invited into the clubhouse. You do need to have certain tools and the knowledge and skill to use them.

You'll employ two primary approaches to getting private money:

Push
Going to investors — meeting investors in social and networking situations

Pull
Bringing investors to you — attracting investors through specific, targeted direct marketing methods

Odds are good that you'll need to employ both tactics; in fact, you'll likely discover some overlap between the two.

Which generates more private money — the Push or the Pull approach — depends on how much private money you need, your existing relationships, your personal strengths, and how much time you commit to your goals.

Before we dive into the specific marketing tactics that will attract private money, let's talk about the tactics that absolutely *won't* land private investors…

The Panhandler

No one does business with a panhandler. A private investor might pity a poor street beggar and hand over some spare change, but he most certainly won't hand over a $500,000 check to a panhandling real estate investor. And he dreads seeing the panhandler coming; he'll be looking for the nearest exit. This is not the first impression (or second or third, for that matter) that you want to create.

You know the panhandler — they guy who trumpets his *need* for private money to anybody and everybody who will listen. If the first and last words out of your mouth are always some variation of a *'gimme private money'* pitch, you're going to have about as much luck as a hot dog vendor at a vegetarian convention.

There's asking for private money and then there's *begging* for private money. Always be aware of that fine line between asking and begging. And don't cross that line — ever. If you do, *you won't get a second chance with that investor.* When you act like the universe will implode if you don't get $50,000 in private money that second, you're guaranteed *not* to get it. Be cool. Be professional (which you *are,* if you're in business for yourself). Don't just *act* like a professional. *Be* a professional.

At a recent real estate investor association meeting, I distinctly remember two guys who accosted every person who entered the room, thrusting flyers on these poor unwitting souls, breathlessly regurgitating their five-minute diatribe about how they needed private money and could 'place their funds' immediately. These clowns might as well have sprayed money repellant all over themselves and approached potential investors wearing sandwich boards that read: "Warning: Stay Away!" Never 'bull-rush' a potential investor. Never act needy. If you follow the strategies in this book, you won't have to act needy because you won't *be* needy.

$$$$ **Resource** $$$$

Enroll in the free 10 week email course to learn more about marketing for private investors. It's critical that you market *yourself and your business* correctly.
Go to *www.TheBookonPrivateMoney.com* and enroll today.

$$$$$$

The Couch Potato

I can virtually guarantee that you won't get private money parked in front of your television. Don't get me wrong, I like to watch a football game or a funny TV show every once in a while, too, but keep the following acronym in mind:

YCDBSOYB

This stands for:

"You Can't Do Business Sitting on Your Butt"

I'm borrowing this from one of my favorite author-mentors, Dan Kennedy. Dan tells the story of a pair of cufflinks his father wore. They were engraved with the letters *YCDBSOYA*.[xi] These cufflinks made a powerful impression on Dan, and served as a lifelong motivator and reminder of the core truth of successful businesspeople: "You Can't Do Business Sitting on Your A**"

Now, in all fairness, there are some successful Internet entrepreneurs who might disagree with this acronym, so perhaps the modern version of the acronym is:

YCDBWTV

You Can't Do Business Watching TV

Trust me: *you will not get private investors watching TV.*

Stay focused on building that pipeline of private investors so that you can turn the spigot on at will. Just because you don't *need* private money this second doesn't mean you should stop working to bring in more. There are many reasons to keep the pipeline full; for example, you may need to cash out a private investor or a great deal may suddenly drop into your lap out of the clear blue sky and you have to react or lose it. You must always be prepared; otherwise, your profits, sooner or later, will be negatively impacted.

The Wild Man

When I first started drumming up private money, I was a wild man, practically beating potential investors over the head with my great investment idea. Why, anyone would be a fool not to invest with me! Then I learned (the hard way) that there were much better tactical maneuvers. *Much* better.

In business, you can choose one of two methods: the hard way or the *smart* way. There's nothing wrong with a hard day's work; you know, the kind of days where you fall asleep the second your head hits the pillow. But here's the thing: You don't make any more money doing it the hard way.

When it comes to creating wealth, you're only worth about $10 per hour from the "neck down"… but tens of thousands times more from the "neck up". There are lots of people, after all, who can match your productivity in terms of manual labor. In business, you make money from the neck up, using your brain-power. Working smart is a neck-up operation. You must become a better user of your brain.

And, working smart when marketing for private money, as you'll see in the next chapter, begins with a KISS.

Chapter 8

KISS – Keep it Simple, S_ _ _ _ _ !

Now, you may be chomping at the bit to get private money. You may be experiencing the urge to scream *Invest with me!* from the rooftops. And you know what? You *should* be excited. You *should* be full of enthusiasm. That positive energy will serve you well. Before you start climbing the ladder to your roof, you should be aware of some obstacles that many real estate investors trip over early on. They're simple, fundamental, and easily avoidable.

John Wooden, the famous UCLA basketball coach who won eleven national championships, was a man who believed in instilling the fundamentals in his players. For instance, he kicked off each season by having his team remove their socks and shoes and pluck the lint from each sock. The rationale: if your feet get blisters, you can't play basketball.[xii]

If you don't get the business fundamentals right, you'll stumble, right out of the gate. Too many investors try to get private money without putting the most basic business marketing fundamentals in place. Big mistake. These fundamentals help stack the private money deck in your favor.

Let's take a closer look…

Naming Your Company
A credible business image doesn't happen by accident. It happens by design. A professional and distinctive company name goes a long way toward establishing trust and credibility. Does the name of your company really have anything to do with attracting private money? It just might. Your company name is one of those little nuts-and-bolts details that affects how private investors perceive you, so put some effort into it. The goal is to stack the deck in your favor.

Your business name is part of the image you want investors to associate with you. The name is the wrapper that contains the investor's impressions of you and experiences with you. They may see or hear your company name before they know anything else about you. When it comes to first impressions, there are no do-overs. You only get one, and getting it right is important.

Create a name that communicates integrity, stability and confidence. Create a name that you can live with in the future. Don't get too trendy. Don't think too small. In addition to building your investors' confidence in you, having a company name that conveys your message and what you do (creating investment opportunity) will boost your own confidence.

One thing to keep in mind: real estate investing is unfamiliar terrain to most people, so avoid using jargon in your company name that a private investor won't immediately grasp. Assume that the investor is hearing about real estate investing for the first time. Avoid 'shock and awe.' You don't want your company name to sound like it belongs in a late-night infomercial.

Compare these company names and their effectiveness on private investors:

Figure 8.1

Private Investor Focused Company Names

Good	Bad
ABC Capital, LLC	Cash 4 Homes, LLC
XYZ investments, Inc	We Buy Houses
Michigan Equities Corp.	Quality Rentals
Blue Water Properties	John Buys Real Estate

It's acceptable to have multiple DBA's (**D**oing **B**usiness **A**s) names associated with your business. For instance, you might present one face of your company as "Cash for Homes" to encourage motivated sellers (a different market from private investors) to contact you, you then present a different, more professional business name to private investors.

You must legitimize the company name you present to investors, so be sure to file the appropriate DBA paperwork with your state. Usually, filing a DBA or creating a new entity is relatively inexpensive, and well worth the cost because it conveys that extra level of legitimacy and credibility. Be sure to consult with a competent attorney before filing. Different states have different DBA rules (which include bank account regulations), and it's easy to make mistakes that could have negative consequences down the road.

Business Cards

A business card is perhaps the most fundamental marketing tool you can have, and one of the most frequently used. Unfortunately, in the real estate investing world, it's also one of the most poorly executed tools. You don't have to present a fancy, high-gloss, whiz-bang business card to your investors. But there are some guidelines you should heed to ensure that your business card performs as effectively as possible.

On the business cards that you present to private investors, be sure to include this information:

- Company Name
- First and Last Name
- Business Address
- Business Phone
- Business Email
- Business Website Address

Keep it simple. There's no need to include three different phone numbers, a fax number, two email addresses and picture of you. Don't clutter the layout. A logo is optional. If you have a logo, make sure it doesn't dominate the entire card layout. Avoid printing anything on the back of the business card — you'll want to leave room for writing in that space.

A simple, uncluttered layout, designed to convey trust, credibility and confidence will be most effective. Remember, your business card always communicates something about you. I recommend using an 80 pt. stock cloth paper business card in a neutral, off-white color. The type should be set in a dark color, such as charcoal gray, black or midnight blue.

Talking About Your Business

When someone asks you what you do for a living, what's your response? Here's how this conversation *usually* goes for most real estate investors…

Private Investor: *"So, what do you do for a living?"*

You: *"I'm in real estate."*

Private Investor: *"Ah, ok great. Anyway…"*

Now, here is how this conversation *should* go:

> Private Investor: *"So, what do you do for a living?"*
>
> You: *"I own a real estate investment company. We specialize in placing private investment capital to purchase distressed residential property."*
>
> Private Investor: *"Really? So, how does that work?"*

See the difference? When talking about what you do for a living or what your business is, speak so that you invite follow up conversation. For example, when asked the "what do you do?" question, answer in a way that is relatable and understandable. The goal of your answer is to invite follow-up questions and comments that will give you an opportunity to explain more about what you do and how you do it.

One great book on this subject is *How to Talk to Anyone: 92 Little Tricks for Big Success in Relationships* by Leil Lowndes. Ms. Lowndes offers many examples of how to talk and interact with people in social settings. I have used many of the techniques she discusses with great success.

Industry Insights

Knowing what's happening in the real estate world will boost your credibility when you're talking to investors. Stay on top of key information such as: interest rates, market prices, vacancy rates, new economic growth initiatives, tax incentives and the major local business headlines. When you know a little bit about what's going on in the business world around you, conversations will be much easier, and you'll make a much better impression.

My private investors have told me on more than one occasion that they really like investing in an upstanding, professional business. That image doesn't happen by accident. It happens by design.

Targeting Investors

No doubt a couple of your most pressing questions right now are: *Who is going to invest with me? How do I find them?* The short answer is: Private investors are everywhere! If you keep your eyes and your ears open, you'll begin to see potential private investors everywhere you go. That neighbor you wave to every morning on the way to work might just be sitting on an inherited fortune. Former colleagues and co-workers, family and friends, real estate agents, mortgage brokers, bankers — they all potentially have money to invest with you, and if they don't, they may know someone who does.

I encourage you to read *The Millionaire Next Door*, written by Thomas Stanley and William Danko.[xiii] This book will open your eyes about who your next private investor might be. You'll never view millionaires the same way again. For example, the average millionaire in America drives a used car, has lived in the same house for many years, and runs his/her own business. What that means is that several people you already know, or will meet in the upcoming weeks and months, have the means and desire to invest with you.

To Get a Private Investor, You Have to Think Like a Private Investor

To get private money, you have to climb inside your investor's mind. Human beings are complicated creatures. We are all alike. And, yet, we are all different. We share common beliefs, motivations and behaviors, but even as our thoughts and behaviors fit into clear patterns, no two psyches are exactly alike, and no two people experience the same event exactly the same way. The investor landscape is comprised of humans who come from many cultures and have different needs, desires, and aspirations.

Start by asking yourself two preliminary questions:

1. What would make this investor uncomfortable about this investment?
2. What potential objections might he or she have to investing with me?

The reason both of these questions are framed in the negative is that most investors will first look for reasons *not* to invest with you before they'll look for reasons *to* invest. How do you overcome these obstacles? Head them off at the pass and remove them from the investor's decision; in other words, explain things thoroughly and remove the perception of risk wherever possible.

---————$$$$ **Resource** $$$$————---
Discover how to save time and money by targeting investors.
Sign up for the free 10 week email course at
www.TheBookonPrivateMoney.com.
---————$$$$$$————---

Eliminate the Risk Factor

While many private investors are always on the lookout for new investments to get excited about, they have a built-in purchase resistance to the unknown — whether the unknown is you or the investment vehicle itself. Often, you'll be competing against other traditional investment vehicles (e.g., stocks, bonds or mutual funds). If you're the "new thing" to the investor, you've got some persuading to do.

People usually buy the products and make the investments that they think they *should* have. To understand this behavioral insecurity, you need to understand how risk is perceived. There are essentially four kinds of risk in every investment decision:

Monetary (Will I lose money?)

Functional (What if the deal doesn't work as advertised?)

Social (Will my peers approve?)

Psychological (Will this make me feel guilty, impulsive or irresponsible?)

Employing the attraction principles of integrity and transparency will go a long way toward helping you create the perception that that investing with *you* is less risky than other options. If you're really lucky (or really clever), your differentiating attribute can eliminate several risks in one blow. For example, having a solid reputation eliminates most of them. Investors are more likely to invest with someone they perceive to be successful and "in-demand." (If everyone else thinks this is the best investment, it *must* be.)

In general, private investors fall into four personality types in terms of how they evaluate information, assess risk, and make decisions:

- **Intuitives**
- **Thinkers**
- **Feelers**
- **Sensors**

Intuitives focus on possibilities, and tend to avoid details. They're big-picture types who love the idea of the "next generation," innovative investment. The intuitive prefers to absorb information in an abstract form — as ideas, images, or concepts. From the initial concept, they'll develop a conceptual framework or structure, into which they can fit the details later.

Thinkers like precision, logic and analytical thinking. They're good at processing details, and are less likely to let emotion "get in the way." Technical details — specifics — appeal to this crowd. The thinker makes decisions based on facts, data and details. They ask questions such as: *What will it cost me? Can I afford it? Will I be sorry tomorrow?*

Feelers make decisions based on feelings, emotions, personal values, and interpersonal relationships. They ask questions such as: *How am I going to feel owning a piece of this property? How am I going to feel driving the new car that the profits will buy me?* They're always susceptible to the feelings of others. They shun intellectual analysis and bend to their personal likes and dislikes. Once they like you, they tend to be loyal partners. They make for good testimonials because their endorsements have an authentic personal style.

Sensors respect concrete facts and have an exceptionally good eye for detail. They prefer details first, building an understanding of the overall concept through the details, step by step. They prefer to learn through the senses — touch, sight, sound, taste and smell. They like to pick things up, turn them over, see all sides. They're adept at establishing context, and perceiving things as they really are. They're rarely wrong.

One of these four investor or "buyer" personalities is almost always dominating any given investment decision. Investors may display characteristics of more than one personality type on any given day. However, people tend to be more comfortable working, learning and functioning as one "type" more often than the others. Even more so when it comes to investing their hard-earned dollars.

Make sure that all your interactions with the investor accommodate the personality type that most closely aligns with your investor's personality traits and decision-making process. Once you've pinpointed the private investor's personality type and removed the perception of risk wherever possible, all that's left is persuading them that your deal — and *you* — are right for them.

Private Investor Persuasion Principles
People often choose to do business with those who stand for ideas that they themselves possess, or want to possess. The following Investor Persuasion Principles are critical to building a private money attraction system:

Affinity. People do business with people (and companies) they like. We're more likely to invest in someone with whom we empathize and feel affinity. When we shop, we choose brands that seem most like us, brands whose personalities align with our own, brands whose image aligns with our own self-image. Personality is your most important ally in your battle to build affinity.

Leadership. People tend to rely on those they perceive to be leaders and authorities. They assume that leading real estate investors must be doing something right, after all — there's a reason why they're the leaders. Establishing yourself as an authority — an expert — on both your market and on the specifics of the private money deals you're presenting will help create the perception that you have leadership qualities.

Consistency. We value consistency in other people, and in the investments we make. The surest way to kill your shot with a private investor is to perform inconsistently. For instance, offering a 10% return on a deal the first time you talk to them, then offering them an 8% return the next time you talk to them. Don't offer benefits when you present a deal, then eliminate or change them before the deal is signed. Don't make claims, then contradict them. Never make promises, then fail to honor them. If you can't deliver on it, don't say it.

Consensus. We humans are social creatures; we tend to seek validation from others. Consensus opinion is an important motivational factor. In any social situation, people tend to observe what other people do in order to decide how to act. (Consider the success of publications such as *Consumer Report* or websites like *Epinions.com* and the degree to which many rely on them to make decisions). Often consensus is built on relatively small, seemingly unimportant aspects of a deal, eventually leading to the tipping point that seals everything. Consensus opinion can also quickly build — or destroy — your reputation in the industry. If a private investor does some checking up on you and the consensus is that you are trustworthy and competent, the investor's mind is eased.

Reciprocity. Most people tend to feel obligated to return a favor. Someone makes a concession hoping for a concession from the other party in return.

It's the age-old concept of "tit for tat" or "stick and carrot," and it's the heart and soul of negotiation. And, make no mistake, every investment decision is a negotiation, even if only in the mind of your prospect. Giving an investor a concession or something free of charge (such as setting up a self-directed IRA for them) is one good way to inspire reciprocity

Scarcity. This is the old First Come, First Served retail technique of creating the perception of "limited quantity." People value what they believe to be scarce or rare. If you let your private investors know that you don't just "let anybody" invest with you or that you have a minimum investment amount, you create an aura of scarcity that will work to your benefit.

Aim for the Right Target

What demographic should you target? Understanding the demographics of a potential investor allows you to tailor all your communications to accommodate his or her specific background, age, profession and financial status. Profiling an investor will not only help you craft your message and presentation, but guide your ongoing relationship with the investor as well.

You'll find it helpful to break investors into the following profiles (note that these investor profiles cross over many different cultures and religions):

- **Established White Collar**
- **Established Blue Collar**
- **Young White collar**
- **Young Blue Collar**
- **Senior**

At first blush, it may seem callous to categorize people in such profiles, but these broad categorizations are simply a practical way to help you develop a strategy for targeting likely prospects and matching the right prospects to the right deals. This broad breakdown of the investors you're likely to deal with is not intended to stereotype individuals. And certainly, there are always exceptions.

Here are some inside tips for working with each type of investor…

Older White-Collar

Your largest source of private money will come from affluent, white-collar individuals. These people are retirees and established professionals (e.g., accountants, lawyers), corporate or government managers. They've historically had high incomes and high savings rates.

More than any other group, older white-collar people tend to focus on their financial position and be more inclined to take action with respect to investing. Most own their own homes; and some may be very affluent. Many have an average net worth in the high six to seven figures or more. Members of this group between the ages of 54 and 70 are *your highest probability target for private investment*. Examples of older white-collar investors might include: doctors, dentists, attorneys, business owners, government/contractors, and business executives.

Established Blue-Collar

The blue-collar demographic is also a good source of private money, though on average, they don't typically have the capital resources of the more affluent established white collar demographic. However, they often do have substantial savings or inheritances to invest. This group has worked in high-paying manufacturing or service jobs, and many own their own home. They typically have low to mid—six figure net-worth. A few may be more affluent, thanks to high-paying jobs and good benefits. Members of this group between the ages of 55 and 65 are a good target. Older blue-collar investors might include: "Big 3" workers, municipal employees, skilled trades people and established contractors.

Younger White-Collar

Dealing with younger investors (ages 25-45) is usually challenging, and does not prove to be fruitful in most cases. This is not to say it can't be done. It's just important to be aware that younger white-collar workers are typically busy building their careers or focused on their families or social activities. They generally haven't accumulated much savings yet; they spend most of what they earn. People who fit this profile may be a good prospective investor for you down the road, and may also be able to introduce you to other potential investors right now. Younger white-collar investors might include: mid-level managers, IT professionals and financial analysts.

Younger Blue-Collar

Younger blue-collar workers (ages 25-45) generally aren't good private investor targets. Their wages don't provide much disposable income. Many are raising families and are focused on other things besides their personal finances.

The savings rates and home ownership rates for this group are low, so pursuing them for investing in your real estate deals is not likely to pan out. Younger blue-collar investors might include: service employees, manufacturing line employees and general laborers.

Senior Investors

Working with senior investors can be challenging but highly rewarding. For the purposes of this book, we'll define 'senior' as any investor over the age of 70. Senior investors sometimes have large sums to invest, but tend to be very conservative. Many live below their means, and actually have the financial resources to subsidize a much higher standard of living than they live.

One concern in dealing with senior investors is that their health status and pending financial needs make it tough for them to commit funds for a long term. Also, their families (children, in-laws, etc.) often become involved in their financial decisions, and family members want to make sure that the senior person is taken care of financially. Be prepared for a committee decision. It's not unheard of for an overly protective family member to suspect that you're trying to take advantage of the senior investor. The important thing to remember is that you have something of value to offer. Be prepared to answer tough questions from family members.

A Word on Spouses

Spouses can occasionally be a stumbling block to closing the deal. Even if the person you're working with is eager and receptive to investing with you, the spouse, either husband or wife, may be more cautious. This is a natural dynamic in many marriages, and is to be expected. In fact, it's quite rare for both spouses to be equally excited about investing with you right off the bat. One usually assumes the role of being "the cautious one."

If you're dealing with a skeptical spouse, be patient! Remember, this is where credibility comes in. Being able to answer their tough questions will satisfy most skeptical spouses and help you close far more private money deals.

Family and Friends as Private Investors

For many real estate investors and entrepreneurs, their first private money investors are family or friends. Family and friends may be your greatest source of moral support. Knowing that they're in your corner throughout the ups and downs that come with owning and operating your own business can play a huge role in your long-term success. I've seen many investors make incredible strides because they had family and friends pulling for them. And there's nothing quite so rewarding as sharing a post-deal victory celebration with your family or some close friends.

I encourage you to consider family and friends for your first source of private money. Some may not have the means or inclination to invest money with you. But others, you may find, are always on the lookout for that next great investment and will appreciate the fact that you considered them. Even though they've been part of your personal "inner circle" for years, they're still looking for a good return on their money. Offer them a sound, no-hassle return, and everybody wins.

You may or may not need to make a formal business proposition to family or friends, depending on the nature of the particular relationship. Either way, treat them with the same level of professionalism you'd show any other investor. Provide the same supporting materials and give the same presentation that you'd use to propose a deal to any other investor.

Often, getting your family and friends to invest with you just requires a simple phone call and sitting down with them to show them your plans. Many novice real estate investors over-complicate and over-think the presentation aspect. Keep it simple. Make it clear. If you truly have a good deal and can clearly communicate that good deal to your family or friends — and you *ask for the investment* — you stand a great chance of getting the money. When talking to family and friends about private money, the most important thing is to be confident and specific about what you want. Once they see that you know what you're doing and are confident in executing your plan, they'll be much more likely to invest with you.

Don't be afraid to accept a smaller investment amount than you originally asked for. For instance, if you're looking for $50,000 for a deal, but your relative or friend only wants to invest $25,000, tell them that if they can firmly commit to investing $25,000, you'll make that investment amount work. Aggressively seek out a deal that *does* work, so that you can get their money invested, even if it's not the deal you first showed them. New real estate investors often miss this first opportunity to get private money rolling into their businesses.

Here are some final guidelines to keep in mind when working with family and friends in a business context:

Professionalism: Always treat family and friends with the same level of professionalism that you would any other private investor.

Proper Care: Take good care of family and friend investors. Make sure you provide statements and notes with business updates. Take them to lunch or dinner and treat them with the respect they deserve for investing with you.

Referrals: Don't neglect the opportunity to ask any family or friends who invest with you to refer other investors. Family and friends can be your most enthusiastic evangelists and bring you lots of new private investors.

Communication: Avoid discussing business on holidays or during other family functions. Establish a separate time and place to discuss business whenever possible.

Time is Money

Have you proposed private money deals before and been brushed off or turned down? As you move forward with your private money goals, make sure you're viewing both the deal and your relationship from the investor's perspective. Qualify your investors *before* you commit time to them. If you don't properly target your investors, you'll be spinning your wheels constantly and getting nowhere fast. You'll waste precious hours presenting your deals to the wrong people, or you'll end up saying the wrong things to the right people.

Part of the key to building a successful real estate business is not wasting time vying for investors who aren't likely to place their funds with you. Your time is valuable. Don't forget that. And other people won't either. Identifying a target market of potential investors who are ready, willing and able to invest will save you countless hours. These hours could be focused on talking to investors who *are* just waiting for the right deal to come along.

Chapter 9

How to *Push* Investors Your Way

Let's cut to the chase: To find private investors successfully and consistently, *you have to put yourself in the way of meeting investors.* You've gotta get out there and meet people. Remember: you have something they want!

Hand to Hand, Face to Face

Don't mistake the push marketing approach as meaning push-*y*. It's really a proactive, face-to-face approach to meeting and attracting investors. You want to place yourself in situations that are conducive to personal contact. Put your business card in their hands and get them on your mailing list. Make sure they remember you and what you do. When they think of real estate, they think of *you*.

Finding investors is a 'contact sport'

It's common for real estate investors to fall for the Silver Bullet Fallacy. They waste so much time trying to find that one silver bullet that will bring them all the private money they could ever want. This shortsighted, tunnel vision approach infects other industries and professions as well. Many businesses rely on just one or two strategies for bringing customers in the door and then they can't figure out where all their customers have gone. There's nothing wrong with sticking to a winning formula, but the winning formula for getting private money will almost always require you to explore many paths. Don't be shortsighted. If you ever start feeling that the time commitment is too great, think about the costlier alternative: No private money and fewer, if any deals.

Many Paths

I would be remiss if I tried to tell you any one surefire way to get twenty investors, but I *can* tell you twenty surefire ways to get one investor. In fact, a multifaceted approach is the most effective strategy for scooping up private investors. Your goal should be to put yourself in front of as many people as possible in as many venues as possible. Here are a few venues that are ripe for the picking:

- Civic Groups & Community Organizations
- Political Groups
- Real Estate Investor Associations
- Charities
- Clubs — Public and Private
- Professionals — Attorneys, Accountants, etc.

Now, you may be protesting, "*I don't have time to get involved with all these groups!*" You don't have to. All you have to do is choose one or two that are full of your target investors. Allocate just a few hours per month with each (unless you're a social butterfly who *wants* to spend more). You'll be amazed how many investors you'll get this way.

Civic Groups & Community Organizations

A great way to meet potential investors is to get involved with community and civic organizations, such as your local Chamber of Commerce, Rotary Club, Lions Club, Kiwanis Club and similar organizations. Participation in these groups shows that you're civic-minded, care about the community, and care about causes other than yourself and your business, which is an endearing quality and rare in business today. And the good news is, more often than not, being a part of these groups doesn't require a major time commitment.

Civic group meetings and other events give you an opportunity to connect with potential investors in a relaxed environment, on a plane that's not "strictly business." It's important to show investors that you're a multifaceted person, that you 'have a life' besides business and — most importantly — that you have *interests similar to theirs*. This is the fast track to building rapport and trust.

Political Groups

Do you vote? Do you care about political issues at all? If so, becoming involved in local political organizations is a great way to meet private investors. Much like civic groups, political groups have a primary objective or purpose that members rally around, which puts you miles ahead on the road to building affinity. Fundraising (e.g., for candidates and elections) is one common purpose of these organizations, and many of the people you'll meet will be good target investors. The prime political fundraising target demographics may also just happen to be *your* primary target market!

Real Estate Investor Groups

Most areas have a real estate investor association (REIA), landlord or property owners group. Investors and real estate industry service providers (e.g., agents, contractors, title companies and mortgage brokers) are frequently involved with these groups, as well. Real estate investor groups are great places to find other like-minded people and private investors.

Where else are you most likely to run into someone who wants to do real estate deals and may have (or know someone that has) private money to invest than a real estate investment-centered group? Go to *www.nationalreia.com* to search for real estate investor groups in your area. Another great resource is *www.meetup.com*.

―――――――――――――$$$$ Resource $$$$―――――――――――――
Real estate investor associations or online forums where
investors come together to learn and network are ideal.
Visit *www.TheBookonPrivateMoney.com* for additional tips.
―――――――――――――$$$$$$―――――――――――――

Charities

Business philanthropy is a prominent networking tool these days, for both large corporations and entrepreneurs alike. Charities, such as the March of Dimes or The American Cancer Society, are a great way to meet potential investors, and give something back to society at the same time. If you've ever been to a charity dinner or auction, you probably noticed that affluent people often attend such events. Many wealthy people donate significant time and money to charities. Golf outings, run/walks, bake sales and other events are great opportunities to meet investors. Getting involved in charity events is also a great way to generate free publicity in your local papers, and free editorial is more valuable than any advertisement you can buy.

Check out organizations in your area and choose one or two that you like. It's not a good idea to join an organization that you *don't* like, purely for the purpose of meeting investors. You'll be more comfortable and more effective in an environment that revolves around a cause you have some passion for.

Working Relationships with Professionals

Professionals such as attorneys, accountants, bankers, real estate agents, mortgage brokers and consultants are good sources of private money because you can "piggyback" their relationships. And they're great referral sources — they possess an inherent credibility, and are thus likely to be instantly believed by people they refer to you.

Attorneys and accountants, in particular, tend to hold sway over their clients. An endorsement from an accountant or an attorney is powerful because the professional has just given *you* de facto credibility. Any initial resistance the investor may have had to meeting with you is largely neutralized by the professional's referral. In other words, their endorsement of you will pre-sell you. You're miles ahead of the game!

How do you get professionals to refer investors to you? Make it a point to tell them what you do and what (who) you're looking for. Be very specific in explaining your value proposition to them.

Now, here's where you may have a bit of leverage with professionals…

Referrals are a two-way street. Professionals rely heavily on referrals to build their businesses. In other words, you can help *them*. Send an attorney or accountant a couple of new clients and it will incentivize them to reciprocate the referral.

Real estate agents and mortgage brokers also have affluent clients who may be interested in investing with you, especially agents and brokers who work with high-end homes or commercial property. The agent or broker may want to do business with you, so they may in turn have a vested interest in referring private investors to you. When agents and brokers understand what you're looking for and they like the deal you're proposing, they can help you connect with private investors.

Always make sure that professionals you come in contact with know what you do and what you're looking for — private money. Communicate to them that you want to establish a working relationship, and that if they can refer an investor, you'll be able to do more business with them. In business, what goes around comes around.

Public/Private Clubs

Public and private clubs offer great opportunities to meet potential investors on an ongoing basis. Clubs open to the public, like your local real estate investor association, are ideal for meeting like-minded people who share your aspirations. You might meet a fellow club member who has the money and inclination to fund one of your deals. Use these events to network. Shake hands, distribute your business card generously, and make sure to follow up with good contacts.

Affluent people tend to congregate at private clubs, such as country clubs or athletic clubs. Associating with affluent individuals greatly increases your odds of meeting someone who has the means and desire to invest with you. One caveat: If you join a private club, don't be in a rush to push your private money proposal. Be cool & confident. Have respect for other members. Some people join the aforementioned clubs to relax and get away from business. Behaving like a panhandler won't help your cause. In fact, you'll likely find that the very people who could become your private investors will flee you, just as they'd flee a street panhandler! It usually takes a little time to establish credibility and acclimate yourself to the club's atmosphere before the right opportunity to broach the subject of business will emerge.

Unless you're rolling in the dough, it probably doesn't make sense to join a private club solely for the purpose of finding private investors. Membership in these clubs is pricey, and doesn't usually cover the cost of the social functions. So, the best advice I can give you is to join for the enjoyment of being a member and let the business naturally follow. Otherwise, you may be better of using that cash to promote yourself in other venues or to invest in your next project.

Getting the Most Out of Getting Out There
So, you're plugged into an organization that's a ripe target for private money… now what? Here are some steps that will help you capitalize on opportunity:

Introduce Yourself to Everyone
Even if you're an introverted person, introduce yourself to everyone you come into contact with at organization events. Always make sure you've got a pocket full of business cards.

Make Sure Everyone Knows What You Do
As you talk to people, work into each conversation a little bit about what you do and how you do it. Don't beat people over the head with a pitch before they're interested in hearing a pitch. Be subtle. People will 'get' it. Be sure that you're casually but continuously positioning yourself as a provider of investment opportunities in real estate. When a potential investor thinks of investment opportunities, they should think of *you*.

Build Your Mailing List
One important aspect of the *Push* approach is critical to building your capacity to maximize the results of the *Pull approach (*which we'll be discussing in the next chapter), and this is: Building your mailing list. I cannot overemphasize this: *Build your mailing list continually.* Get contact information for each

person you meet, either by asking for a business card or through other means, such as a membership directory or group mailing list. You may also simply be able to ask for their contact information on the premise that you would like to add them to your Christmas mailing list (which you will).

Ask for Referrals

There is a difference between being needy for private money and asking people you meet to refer you to someone who may be interested in investing with you. For example: "Jim, I'm raising capital for a real estate deal. If you know anyone who'd be interested in earning twelve percent on their money, would you give me their contact information, or have them contact me?"

By asking someone you've identified as a good target investor if *they* know anyone who might be interested in investing with you, you're indirectly asking *that* person if they're interested as well. Undoubtedly, the person whom you asked for the referral from will want more information, which gives you a great opportunity to qualify them as an investor.

Private money will not magically show up in your mailbox, no matter how much you may want it to. It's going to require a little effort from you. Get out there and start pushing people toward it. "Mixing and mingling" is never as hard as you fear. The more involved you get, the more people you know, the quicker word about you will spread. Ultimately, involvement will bring investors to you.

Chapter 10

How to *Pull* Investors Toward You

Both the *Push* and *Pull* approaches are strategies that will put you on the path of least resistance to getting private investors running to grab their checkbooks. The *Pull* approach uses marketing media to create a force field that attracts private money while you sleep. (now, *that's* working smart!)

You'll create this magnetizing force through two primary paths: Online marketing and offline marketing.

Harness the Power of the Web

The Internet has become an integral part of the fabric of our everyday lives. You must harness the power of the Internet to attract interest from private investors. Your business website, blog, social media and online forums can connect you to investors. These media are some of the most cost-effective promotional avenues available — they have the potential for the highest exposure for the lowest cost — often free, except for the cost of your time. Perhaps best of all, they're hard at work for you while you're sleeping.

The Website

A high-quality website is a critical component of becoming a private money magnet. Your website will be a golden opportunity to showcase investment opportunities and open a dialogue with potential investors. The website — done well — establishes rapport, builds credibility and helps pre-sell both you and the idea of investing with you.

You must have a website that caters specifically to private investors. So, if, for example, you already have a company website that targets customers (e.g., renters, home buyers, etc.) you must build a separate and distinct website that targets private money.

Here's a quick summary of why you must have a private investor focused website…

1. **Credibility.** Simply put: You must have a website because you're expected to. These days, it's assumed that any company worth its salt will have a website. If you don't, investors may be suspicious of you.

With no website, you'll be starting from a position of weakness, and you'll have to work that much harder to establish credibility. A good website will meet the investors' initial requirement for information about your company.

2. **Communicating Your Message.** Your website allows you to continue communicating with your investors when you're not with them in person. It's a tool that helps them evaluate who you are and what you've got to offer. These days, we're conditioned to use the Internet to do our homework before purchasing or investing — whether it's a house, a flat-screen television, or a tropical vacation. Your private investors will be no different. Accept this 'investigate before you buy' mindset and integrate it into your marketing strategy. Use that opportunity to present information that will presell you.

3. **Reinforcing Your Message.** Your website can reinforce what you tell investors in person, by phone and in email. It's important to get this right. For example, let's say you tell your investors that you invest in multi-family properties. If your website includes photos of apartment buildings and samples of apartment building deals, you connect the dots for the investor and reinforce message consistency. Conversely, if you tell an investor that you invest in apartment buildings and your website only features single-family house deals, your investor will be confused, perhaps even suspicious, and your credibility is diminished.

4. **Presenting Information.** Websites can present information in a visually stimulating and controlled format. You have total control of what you say and how you say it. You can put your best foot forward and make a great first impression. You can present your company philosophy, business outlook, and compelling reasons for investing with you.

5. **Gathering Information.** Your website can be a tool to help you gather information from potential investors. A web contact form allows interested parties to provide information so that you can follow up with them and see if there's a match. This can be especially important in a scenario where you meet an investor in a social situation, give them your business card (which includes your website URL) and they later visit your website. A quick and easy contact form can encourage them to input information such as their name,

email address and phone number, which then gives you an opportunity to follow up multiple ways. Your contact form could also, for example, trigger an auto-responder email which provides information about your company or a particular investment opportunity.

6. **Referral.** A website is a great source for referrals. Once someone has invested with you and happy with the result, they may feel like showing you off to their family and friends. Certainly, you'll be happy to oblige! They might send your website URL to friends, colleagues or other interested parties.

Constructing Your Website

Let's talk about some of the most important aspects of a private investor-focused website:

The Domain Name

Put some time and effort into choosing a good domain name. The domain is the information following the "www."; for example, in http://www.XYZCapital.com, "XYZCapital.com" is the domain. Be sure to use your own domain name in your primary email address; for example, "John@XYZcapital.com". It's a credibility-builder and it will look much more polished and professional on your business cards and promotional pieces than "John@yahoo.com." Free email accounts are fine for personal use, but use your own domain name for business.

Using a domain such as Yahoo® or Hotmail®, makes you look unprofessional or cheap. You can buy a domain name for around $10 per year, and hosting plus email services for less than $100 a year. This is a small price to pay. Register your own domain name as soon as possible, if you haven't already done it. Reliable registrars that offer reasonable pricing and instant registration include: *Godaddy.com* and *1and1.com*. These two are my personal favorites. You can easily set up web e-mail accounts through these companies (using your domain), as well. The administration interface is simple and quick — you don't have to be a tech whiz!

---—————————$$$$ **Resource** $$$$———————————
Get a Private Money Magnet website today.
Visit www.MyPrivateMoneyWebsite.com
—————————————$$$$$$————————————————

Aesthetic

Design a first-class website — crisp, clean, and simple. Your goal is to look reputable, credible and established. You want to look like you're in the investment business, not the late-night-infomercial-get-rich-quick business.

You want the investor to walk away assuming that you're profitable, as opposed to looking like you're too poor or too cheap to build a quality website. Your website should meet or exceed the investor's expectations. Remember, your website may be an investor's first impression of you, your first opportunity to build trust and credibility. Your website can help get you a meeting. It can even help persuade a skeptical spouse or overcome potential objections.

Content

Your website's content should inform and generate interest. It should help confirm and reinforce any dialogue you may have already had with investors. Avoid using jargon or terms that the average person may not understand or language that may cause confusion. A good rule of thumb when you write is to put yourself in the shoes of someone who has never heard of you or what you do.

Navigation

Your website should be easy to navigate. Visitors shouldn't have to second-guess your buttons — a click should give them what they expected to get. And try to follow the two-click rule: Visitors shouldn't have to click more than two levels deep to reach their destination page, and preferably only one click.

Images

Choose your images and pictures carefully. Don't use images that could leave an unfavorable impression. For example, if you show pictures of flashy or ostentatious lifestyles, like exotic cars and boats, you may create the impression that you're a 'get rich quick' schemer, not a serious, credible real estate investor. Don't show pictures of giant piles of money that look like they might have been confiscated in drug raids. Consider using images that are symbolic of business situations, such as two people smiling and shaking hands, or people dressed in business attire. Use images of properties from actual deals that you've done wherever possible, especially if they symbolize the kinds of deals you'd like to do more of.

Offering Information

If you're offering information in the form of a report or prospectus, be sure it's available in a format that allows for easy reading and is safe on all computer platforms — Acrobat PDF format is your best choice. I prefer to require visitors to complete a contact information form in order to either receive a link to download the file or a reply email with the report attached. Typically, the information I provide in response to receiving contact information is a company brochure or pictures and information about recent deals. This strategy gives the site visitor a chance to know you and your company better.

Capturing Information

Your website must include a form to capture contact information. A "contact" page with an information form box is ideal. All information submitted will be captured in your email or, if you prefer, a back-end database or contact management system. Be sure to follow up with all requests for information in a timely manner.

Website Disclaimer

To stay on the right side of the securities regulators, be sure to include a disclaimer on your website that tells any visitor that the information on your site is "not an offer to purchase or sell securities and that any securities will only be offered under registration or an appropriate exemption." There may be other disclaimers that your particular site may need. Ask your attorney to provide the appropriate disclaimer language for your site.

Driving Traffic to Your Website

There are many ways that you can drive traffic to your website. The key is to drive *qualified* hits to your website. You want visitors to spend time learning about your business and your opportunity. The ultimate goal is to get them to contact you because they want to invest some money.

Pay-per-click (PPC) advertising, such as using Google Adwords© or banner ads on targeted sites where your private investors might be surfing can be extremely effective in getting good hits to your site. Another valuable technique is to have other websites link to your website. This way, a visitor on another website can just click over to yours in an instant. You can accomplish this by posting articles or comments on other people's websites or blogs (if allowed) that include your website link or you can ask other website owners to link to your site.

Blogs

Think of a blog as an online journal. It should be separate and distinct from your private money-focused website. ('*Blog*' is an abbreviation of the word "*Weblog*") Blogs have become a widely accepted medium for anyone to communicate their opinions, thoughts, and feelings on any subject — from world class journalists and politicians to everyday people, from business to personal topics.

Blogs are a great platform for posting audio, video, educational articles, opinions, and announcements. Blogging can be effective because it's a more casual environment for communicating what's going on in your business or your opinions on relevant real estate investment subjects.

Some blog hosts allow you to set up a free blog (Google®'s Blogspot®, for example) and start posting in a matter of minutes. It's that easy. Type in a few thoughts about a particular subject and distribute your thoughts to the world in seconds. Glancing at the business headlines on any given day can inspire you to write something relevant about the economy or the real estate market. Be creative. Your posts don't have to be long or complicated. Sometimes a paragraph or two will do the trick.

A blog provides you and your business with an additional online presence beyond the website, and can effectively build increased interest in you and what you have to say. It also increases the likelihood that your name will surface in search engine results.

Avoid writing blog posts that are inflammatory, politically polarizing, or overly socially or religiously opinionated as this may alienate more people than you attract! Don't post potentially embarrassing words or pictures. You never know who might read your blog. Remember, the goal of your blog is to attract private money, so don't risk offending potential investors.

Social Media
People of all ages are getting involved in social networking sites (even my grandmother is on *Facebook*®!). Millions in advertising dollars are being poured into social media, and the potential reach is far and wide. Social media connects you with new people. You can communicate the fact that you invest in real estate and are looking for investors. You can provide updates on your business and mention recent milestones. For example, you can let those connected to you know that you've completed a deal, or that you need a new tenant. The possibilities are endless!

The biggest benefit of social media is that it allows messages, videos or breaking news to pass 'virally' or quickly from one person to the next — much faster than through traditional means. So, if someone you know is interested in one of your business opportunities, the people they know and the people that those people know (and so on and so on) will see it as well. This ripple effect is powerful.

Social media sites like Facebook®, LinkedIn® and MySpace® are ideal for connecting with friends, former classmates, relatives and business colleagues. LinkedIn® is the top site for connecting business associates. Facebook®, currently the dominant force in social media, was initially a venue for college students, but has evolved into a much broader platform. Let's go through some of these social media outlets in more detail.

Facebook®

Facebook® (www.facebook.com) is a social media website that connects you to family, friends, co-workers, former classmates or pretty much anybody else in the world. These connections are called "Friends." On Facebook®, you can see status updates from your friends (what people are doing at a given point in time), view pictures and videos and also communicate by writing personal messages or using the instant message service.

One of the most unique things about Facebook® is that is has a special tool that makes friend suggestions to you based on the criteria you enter on your profile and other Facebook® friends you have. For instance, if you graduated from James Madison High School in 1988, the site will help connect you with other people that you went to high school with or who attended the same school.

Facebook® also allows you to create a 'fan' page, a public page through which you can promote your business in any number of ways. You can attract 'fans' (many of whom may be existing friends) to your fan page, and these fans can be kept abreast of everything you post. Post videos and marketing messages on your fan pages — be creative. Don't be afraid to post potential deals for private investors (there are some legalities to be considered with this, which we'll cover in a later chapter).

LinkedIn®

LinkedIn® is an online business networking community that makes connecting with business colleagues and associates free and easy. Go to www.LinkedIn.com and start building your network right away. All you need to set up an account is an email address. Once you complete your profile, you can invite your business contacts to 'connect' with you and join your LinkedIn® network.

One unique feature of LinkedIn® is the ability to see the connections of people you're connected to — it's sort of like taking a peek at someone's Rolodex. It's the modern, electronic way to spur introductions and develop new business relationships. You can use LinkedIn® to mine for prospective investors and get introductions to them through your connections. Look for good matches, based on occupation and location, and ask your mutual acquaintances for an introduction. You can recommend or endorse people with whom you've done business, and others can endorse you. Endorsements create a referral for all to see.

As your contacts make new connections, those connections are posted, which allows you to investigate new connection possibilities on an ongoing basis.

LinkedIn® also has an "Answers" section, which allows anyone to post questions on various business subjects, and the entire community can offer answers. People who post informative answers get noticed, which can trigger new connections and relationships. You could, for example, post a question about where to find private money for a deal.

Twitter®
Twitter® is best defined as a 'micro-blog' that allows you to communicate short messages of 140 characters or less, which are called 'tweets' to those who "follow" you. Twitter® allows you to follow just about anyone who has a Twitter® account. Following is simply viewing the tweets of someone else that is using the service. You can follow the tweets of famous actors, athletes, entertainers and politicians. President Obama's campaign, for example, utilized Twitter® to mobilize voters and supporters in the 2008 presidential election.

Signing up for Twitter® is free and easy. Go to www.twitter.com and sign up for an account. During the signup process, you have the option to invite others to follow you and to elect to follow people you know, or people already using Twitter® who are in your contact list.

The best use of Twitter® for you may be posting short messages that alert your followers to interesting websites, or for posting thoughts other like-minded individuals may find amusing. Building a loyal rapport is important – be interesting. Tweet about a deal you have. Being straightforward is usually the best way to get results. There are no real rules on Twitter®, but you're likely to be more successful if you don't focus solely on promoting your business; tweet about other things, as well. Best not to be a one-sided tweeter, or you may lose followers.

Some Final Tips for Using Social Media
Don't be shy about selling yourself, but don't go overboard. Promote your business with class and strive to add value when participating in these mediums. Post comments, resources and links that people will find interesting and relevant, and that will continue to build your credibility and, ideally, establish you as a leader. Keep your messages fresh. Messages can grow old and tired quickly; remember, the same people (those connected to you) see it each time you post.

Search Engine Presence

In addition to gaining direct exposure, social media participation and your business website can also increase your visibility in the search engines (e.g., Google®, Yahoo®, Bing®) and help you build a stronger internet presence. The search engine results pages (SERPs) are the best way for people to find your business on the Web, particularly Google®, which owns the largest market share of search engine traffic.

For example, if someone is searching for the keyword phrase "real estate investing" and clicks one of your pages in the search results, you generate traffic to your website or blog and more credibility as a result of having a presence in the SERPs. The more SERPs you get, the more ubiquitous you seem. The more ubiquitous you seem, the more credible you seem, and the more you seem to the searcher that you're a market leader. (It's a variation of the Consensus persuasion principle: If Google® thinks you're worthy of ranking in the SERPs, you must be a leader.)

You should know that many people who take your business card will "Google" you. Having a website, blog, and a social media presence that effectively (and repeatedly) uses relevant keywords such as "real estate investing" and "private money investment" can help boost your ranking in the SERPs.

Offline Marketing

Some real estate investors focus their marketing dollars solely online. An online-only approach may work in some instances, but ultimately, it's very limiting — a tunnel vision approach to marketing. There are many tactics that can pull investors toward you. Why not hedge your bets? Despite the fact that we live in an increasingly electronic world, offline marketing and communications can still be a highly effective route to getting private investors; in fact, just as effective as online marketing.

A big part of your offline marketing success will be driven by your ability to build a mailing list from personal contacts. Add every one of your contacts to your mailing list, without exception. While there are many offline marketing methods to choose from (e.g., direct mail, place ads, yellow pages, etc.), the following techniques have proven extremely effective for me:

- **Company Newsletter**
- **Personal Correspondence**
- **Testimonials**
- **Direct Mail & Advertising**

Company Newsletter

Developing a print newsletter for your real estate business is one of most important marketing tactics you can implement. People love receiving personal mail and they appreciate free, valuable information. A simple two to four page newsletter with information about your company and helpful real estate information (e.g., tips on selling your home) provides value to the potential investor and works to establish *you* as an authority in your industry. Authority helps build the credibility necessary to persuade private investors to fork over six-figure checks.

In each newsletter, there are a few things you must include: subtly let the reader know that you are currently accepting new investors for projects. A great way to get a few hundred grand in new private money is to include before-and-after shots of a completed project on the front page alongside a photo of you with your investor as well as a testimonial from the investor.

A monthly newsletter will probably yield the best results, but a quarterly newsletter can also be effective. Be consistent with your mailings. If it's a monthly newsletter, mail it monthly; if it's a quarterly newsletter, mail it quarterly.

Your newsletter should always include some of the following aspects:

- Local real estate market information (you could obtain this information from a real estate agent or online through sources such as www.RealtyTrac.com)
- Tips for homeowners (examples: preparing your home for winter, making your lawn greener, saving energy)
- Your company contact information (mandatory to have and must be prominently displayed)
- Photos of deals you're working or have completed
- Your company mission/vision statement

Be creative. Have fun. You'll quickly find that your newsletter will become an important communication tool.

Personal Correspondence

Think personalized letters and hand-addressed mailings are old-fashioned? Well, it may be old school, but, for me, it's been known to result in hundreds of thousands of dollars in private money investment within weeks of launching a campaign.

Here's how it works: once you target specific investors or referral sources for private money, you begin sending them handwritten or neatly typed (but personally-signed) mail pieces. Now, these pieces are not hokey, blind-list junk mail. They're personally tailored to each reader and designed to elicit a specific response — that's the key. For example, a letter to someone you recently met at a Chamber of Commerce function and tell them that you enjoyed meeting them and would like to get together with them in the near future to show them your business and some investments.

The main reason this approach works is that people *love* getting personal mail. Most of us simply don't get personal mail anymore (except bills). When you hand-address an envelope or send personal correspondence, the open-rate is much higher, and the likelihood of response is much higher, too. Often, people will call you just to thank you for sending them a letter (even though the letter was building your case for a private money investment!).

Make it a point to send personal correspondence to every single target investor or referral source you meet — it'll take maybe 15-20 minutes per day. This method has paid off for me to the tune of at least a *$1,000,000 return on my investment.* Not a bad return, eh?

Testimonials
I know what you're thinking: *"Testimonials? Those are only for home shopping shows and get-rich-quick marketers!"* Not true. The sad truth is that everyone has a high level of skepticism about *everything* these days. This is true in business and perhaps no sector inspires a higher level of skepticism than the investment market. It's almost impossible to sell yourself as persuasively as somebody else can sell you.

A written or video testimonial is a powerful communication tool. A testimonial from someone you've done business with (*especially* a satisfied private investor) puts you *miles* ahead in the path to persuasion. Testimonials can be particularly important for real estate investors who are just starting their businesses, and haven't done any private money deals yet.

Collect testimonials from:
- Private investors who have invested, or are currently investing with you (this is a gimme!)

- Your real estate agent (about how they enjoy working with you)
- A contractor (about how you're a good person to do business with)
- A co-worker (someone who can attest to your competence and work ethic)
- Anybody else who will say good things about you (business-related testimonials are most effective)

Powerful testimonials, even those that aren't from private investors, will help you close more private money deals than you otherwise would have. Contrary to what you might think, most people are very open to giving testimonials if they've had a positive experience with you. You can use testimonials in a company brochure, on your website or in your newsletter and other promotional materials.

Legal Alert

You knew the legal-speak was bound to pop up at some point, didn't you? But when you're dealing with other people's money (OPM), many of your actions fall within the scope of Securities Laws. As entrepreneurs, we might dislike the miles of red tape we have to deal with these days. Certainly, some of it's necessary to organize our society and create a safer, more profitable business environment. But much of it is purely and simply annoying bureaucracy.

There are a few legal basics you need to know when advertising for private money. You must take care to comply with securities laws that apply to advertising and promotional activities. Virtually all advertising you do for private money is subject to securities laws, and as a business owner, it's your responsibility to know the laws and conduct your business within the scope of those laws. Ignorance of the law is not an excuse. We'll cover securities laws in more depth later.

Direct Marketing & Advertising

If you're going to advertise to bring private investors to you, it's best if you go about it the right way. This means that you'll have to focus on putting a good marketing campaign together. Sounds easy, right? Not exactly.

There isn't a good company, big or small, that doesn't spend a great deal of time devising ways to bring customers in the door. When you start advertising for private money, you have to become a good marketer for investors. However, you're not alone. You won't be the only one advertising for investment dollars.

There is a lot competition from Wall Street firms and local financial planners alike. Everyone seems to want a piece of your private investors' portfolio.

It's easy to take the marketing part for granted when it comes to private money. I often come across investors who want to advertise for private money and feel that if they simply hang out a shingle offering 12% secured returns that they'll have more leads than they can count. This is far from the truth. I've advertised for private money using the "12% secured returns" route and had tepid results at best. You need to offer something more compelling and conscientiously market *your* offer to a hungry audience.

When you advertise for private money, you should have a sound marketing campaign in place. This campaign should include proper lead generation, follow up sequences, and a unique offer. Skip any one of these components and you're going to be wasting a lot of time and money.

Advertising for private money, such as with an Internet landing page or a place ad in a newspaper should be used as lead generators. You want to gain the interest of a prospective investor so that they contact you to learn more about what you're offering. Once the prospect contacts you, you must have something to offer them, such as an informational brochure or other company information. From there, you must have a unique offer to bring them into the fold as a good prospective investor.

One of the biggest challenges you'll run into here is how to get people to read your ad and then respond. I think it's best to gain the attention of prospective investors with approaches that are not widely used by traditional financial planning or asset management firms. You must stand out and you must have a unique selling proposition.

For instance, in the stock market downturn of fall 2008- spring 2009, one approach that gained attention for me was offering how to show people a way to protect their nest egg from market turmoil *without* pushing their target retirement date out an additional five or ten years. Private investors in the 55-65 age group responded favorably to this approach.

Carefully consider what you will do when an investor calls you or contacts you from your website. Will you be meeting with them to present a deal? Will you be inviting them to an educational event? You should have the entire sequence planned out from the beginning. Remove as much guess work for yourself as possible.

Whichever advertising route you take, make sure that you can carefully track the results and compare them with your expenditures. If you purchase a mailing list, you are going to want to know what your return on marketing dollars is, especially when the cost of the list, mailings and follow up marketing is considered. Thinking in terms of ROI is not just limited to real estate deals – you must apply this to your entire business.

Stoke the Flames...
Focused, continual effort is the key to getting private investors, for both the *Push* and *Pull* approaches. Being aggressive with your marketing will reward you with so many private investors you won't know what to do with all of them! Remember, keep your foot on the gas. Even as you're successfully landing investors, keep working to fill that pipeline. Now that you know how and where to find private investors, Part IV will show you how to get them to write the check.

PART IV

Seal the Deal

Now that you know how to attract private money and how and where to meet investors, the next thing you need to know is what the heck to do once you have them eager to invest in your deals. You need to know how to propose deals to private investors, get them to say "YES!"- and I mean get them to actually jump out of their chairs and write you a check. You must then know how to properly close the deal.

One of the best feelings I've ever had in business has been getting a huge private money check. There is nothing like it. It's a complete rush. A natural high. It's one of the things that gets me out of bed in the morning and eager to tackle the day. Unfortunately, if you don't get this part right, a whole lot of hard work and time spent getting investors will be wasted. I don't want you to be the investor that gets the ball all the way down to the two-yard line only to fumble before taking it to glory.

You have to be careful about how you propose meeting with investors and how you ask for their investment dollars. One wrong move and the investor will write you off for a long time. It's really hard to make a second go around at a private investor that you've hit up to invest with you.

A Difficult Lesson
One time at a real estate group meeting in my area, I was talking to a guy I thought was perfect for investing with me. He had the money and the inclination to do it. He even alluded to investing some funds into real estate in prior conversations. One night, determined to make him one of my investors, I strolled up and began a conversation. Things went well up until it came time for me to dip my toe in the water. Except, I dove right in — like diving into a pool when you don't know how deep it is — not a good idea. Anyway, I made some awkward attempt at asking him if he wanted to sit down and discuss investing with me and he puckered right up and looked away. He quickly excused himself and made like a tree. I was left standing in the same spot, feeling my limbs go numb.

"What is something I said?" I asked myself. Well, I never really found out exactly what I said that turned that particular private investor off, because it

actually ended up being something I *didn't say*. When it comes to private money, the little things count – big time. You have to know how to present and propose a deal the right way, or you may not get a chance with a private investor. I hate to make it out to be a 'make or break' thing, but unless you have something compelling for someone, they will be reluctant to sit down with you again to look at the very same thing because you simply have found the correct way to present it.

Another big pain point for me when I first got started with private money was that I was continually getting sit-down meetings with prospective investors and not walking away with a check in my hand (or even a commitment to invest in a deal). I kept getting the "well, I'll think about it," response after almost every meeting. Needless to say, this was extremely frustrating. I was almost to the finish line and could not seem to cross it.

Sand in Your Face
To help you avoid getting sand kicked in your face, the remainder of this section we will cover four key aspects to getting private money

- How to get the meeting
- How to propose the deal
- What rate of return to pay
- How to close the deal

These are the most critical aspects you need to have down as you build your horde of private investors. Skip over any one of them and you may find yourself like I did on more than one occasion - wondering what went wrong. This entire section of the book will show you exactly what to do so all of your efforts pay off.

Chapter 11

Getting the Meeting

Thus far, you've marketed yourself to potential investors, and now you've got a prospect...Your next step is to get a meeting so that you can present your deal. There are two ways that you can present your opportunity: one-on-one or to a group of investors. Each meeting format has pros and cons and differences in how to follow up properly. It is highly unlikely that you're going to build significant amounts of private money being an anonymous blip on a computer screen. You need to get a meeting so you can get the money.

Choosing a Meeting Format

In order to propose a meeting, you must have a format in mind. More specifically — you need to know the scenarios in which you will present your opportunity to the private investor *before* proposing it. The meeting format you use, either one-on-one or group, will depend on factors such as your pre-existing relationship with the investor and the type of deal you are proposing. Your personal preference and comfort level enter into the picture as well. Many people aren't comfortable with public speaking and this discomfort may be enhanced with the thought of speaking in front of people that may invest hundreds of thousands or even millions of dollars with you. I will discuss both meeting formats and my experiences with each in this chapter.

The One-On-One Meeting

In my experience, the face-to-face, mano-e-mano meeting is the best way to get the investment. You now have a chance to forge a more intimate connection. The investor can shake your hand, look you in the eye and, hopefully, decide that they're investing with someone they can trust.

Getting the Meeting
How should you propose the meeting? What language should you use? Well, there's no one magical line that will work with every investor. How you propose the meeting usually depends on how you set the table beforehand.

Timing is important. If you've laid the groundwork properly... if you've enticed them to ask questions and made them feel comfortable about your answers... if they've expressed interest in investing with you, propose a meeting.

There will be a right moment. When you call or email them to propose meeting to discuss an investment deal, it shouldn't be a total surprise to them.

Scheduling appointments is more effective by phone than email. In a phone conversation, you can adjust and counter dates and locations in mere seconds, but it can take a flurry of emails to accomplish the same thing, and you may lose precious days waiting for a response. Plus, a phone call gives you one more opportunity to speak to the prospective investor, one more rapport-building opportunity.

Here are a couple of sample scripts that you can use to propose a meeting:

> "John, I have a deal coming up that I think you'd be interested in investing in, based on our previous conversations. When are you available to take a look at the details?"

> "Sue do you remember when we discussed how we partner with investors like you in our real estate business? Well, I have a deal that I think we can work on together. Can I go over the details with you? You can then tell me your level of interest."

If you've ever worked in sales, you probably recognize something familiar in these examples. You are *presuming* that they're interested unless they tell you otherwise. This technique also helps screen prospects. You can assess the prospect's level of interest before you put more time into working with them.

Avoid giving too much information about the deal over the phone or in email. Prospective investors will almost certainly ask you to go over some of the details when you first propose a meeting. What's the solution? Tell them: "It's just a little complicated to go into over by phone, so I prefer to sit down with you so that I can *show* you all the details."

If the investor continues to press for more information, give them the basics. For instance, reveal the location, the type of deal, and the anticipated return. Then pointedly ask if they're interested in learning more and propose the meeting again. Make sure you lock your investor down to a specific time and location. Most people are busy and any time commitment can be a challenge.

Location, Location, Location…for the Meeting!
Location will be critical to the success of your meeting. I find that quiet meeting places, like a coffee house or a small restaurant is ideal. And here's a

little-known secret: Avoid meetings that involve food! Now, this may sound strange, but food tends to get in the way of a productive proposal. The task of eating a meal actually distracts both parties from the overall purpose of the meeting, and it always takes more time, so you're burning up more of your time, as well as your investor's time.

Schedule constraints also make meal-meetings less than ideal for investors. For example, if your prospective investor has a full time job, and you schedule a lunch meeting, they usually only have 30 to 60 minutes for lunch; some of which is spent commuting to and from the meeting location. Part of the meeting will be devoted to small talk and exchanging pleasantries, as well as food and drink ordering. That leaves little time for talking about the deal. You're painting yourself into a corner. You won't be able to effectively propose your deal.

If you have no other option than meeting over food, dinner is a better choice than lunch. People usually have more time to eat dinner, and tend to be more relaxed. Another problem with lunch meetings is that the investor has to go back to their workday. When they head back to work, your proposal has a fairly high chance of slipping to a lower slot on their priority list.

Since lunch meetings may be unavoidable, if you must do a lunch meeting, choose a quiet location that's low-key, low-traffic and offers fast, courteous service. You want to be sure you'll be able to hear each other talk. Don't get trapped in a loud, bustling environment that can only detract from the meeting.

When?
The best times for meeting with potential private investors are late morning, or mid-afternoon. The most effective time slots are: 10:00 am, 11:00 am, 3:00 pm, or 4:00 pm. These times give your investors a little wiggle room in their schedules. They can either let the meeting run into their lunch hour, or let it run to the end of their workday.

Don't Forget to Confirm the Meeting!
Once you've gotten the investor to agree to the time and place, be sure to *call the day before to confirm the meeting*. Calling to confirm respects everyone's time. This is very important; you don't want to get stood up, or worse, stand up your investor. Sometimes, things come up at the last minute. And occasionally prospects will not be respectful of your time. But scheduling conflicts do happen.

Remember, it's *you* who is asking something of *them*. People are busy with work, family and other commitments, so make *sure* they can attend your meeting. Confirm the time and location as well. If the investor is unsure or suggests that they may not be able to make it, try to reschedule for another date that works for everyone. And always invite the investor's spouse to the meeting.

Group Presentations (aka "Investor Receptions")
Although meeting with investors one-on-one has been most effective for me, I have also had good success when presenting my investment opportunities to groups of prospective investors. I like to call these meetings "receptions."

Presenting to a crowd of 15-20 investors that each may invest $50,000-$100,000 or more with you is exciting. The sheer dollar volume of investment capital is enough to get your blood pumping! This type of meeting environment adds a layer of pomp and circumstance and builds more credibility for you. After all, you've taken the time, money, energy and effort to orchestrate this event – these things resonate in the investor's minds. Also, like most people, private investors like to be 'wined & dined' — made to feel special. When you combine all of these factors, you have a recipe for big success.

On the flip side, there are more variables to consider when you are presenting to a group of investors than there are with a one-on-one meeting. You need to identify and obtain your attendees, select a venue and prepare a presentation and materials. In addition, you must also have carefully planned follow-up steps for after the meeting to maximize its effectiveness. There are the costs to consider when doing a reception as well.

Let's discuss more details of a successful reception:

The Invitation
Out of the different variations I have tried, your best starting point will be to identify an attendee list and then send invitations to them. Treat it as if it was an important event, like a wedding (without the black tie or gift bearing requirements). This gives you the best shot at your event being taken seriously (which it should) and getting a good response. Give some event specifics on a separate card insert. I like to include some basic information on my company and a brief description of the investment opportunity that will be discussed. Keep it simple.

Generally, people don't get a ton of invitations to events, so yours will stand out. Since you'll be spending time and money on a group presentation, send attractive, formal invitations and… RSVP. The RSVP assures that they'll take the meeting more seriously and you can better control costs if you know how many people will be attending. Strongly encourage your invitees to bring a guest. They'll be more comfortable about attending if they can bring along someone they know. In fact, make it obvious that you expect them to bring somebody. This helps boost your meeting attendance as well and enlarges your investor pool.

Assemble your group carefully. Ideally, you want to present to a group of investors who know each other, or are at least familiar with each other and may share common interests. A better group dynamic makes for a better ambiance. You don't want people to feel like they're among strangers. So, for instance, you might assemble a few former co-workers that you've qualified as good investor candidates, or members of a club that you belong to, or organization you are involved in.

**This is the power of the *Push* approach. When you are out meeting and getting acquainted with people in organizations like your Chamber of Commerce or a charity, you are building a great reception attendee list. **

Location, Location, Location…for the Reception!
Set yourself up for success by selecting a nice venue and making sure that the entire event — from invitation to conclusion — is as professional as possible.

The best location will be contingent on the size of the group. For smaller groups of 4 to 5 people, you may be able to reserve a private room at a nice local restaurant. For larger groups, you may need to reserve a banquet facility that can accommodate and service a bigger group.

Cost can be a factor when selecting the venue. You don't want to be too frugal, or you'll look cheap or unprofitable — neither is good. You may not be able to afford the Ritz, but make sure the venue you choose conveys the image and creates the ambiance that you want your investors to experience. The location *will* be part of the experience they remember when they're considering your deal.

Here are some suggestions for meeting locations:
- Country Club
- Banquet Hall
- Private Club
- Private Section of Restaurant
- Hotel Meeting Rooms

Be sure to iron out all the details with the venue ahead of time. If you need some help, consider hiring an event planner. The cost of your venue will depend on many factors — including whether you provide food and beverages, the day of the week and the number of attendees. Plan on spending at least $500 to $3,000.

With investor receptions, I have had success hosting evening events with dinner included as well as events that were just 'mixers' with drinks and appetizers served. Your personal preferences, your attendee size and venue will dictate your decision here. It really depends on what format will make *you* the most effective and give you the most 'punch' with your attendees.

For instance, people that are used to going to the type of functions that you are hosting, such as high net worth individuals or professionals, may appreciate the efforts of the event, but want something more 'cut to the chase.' Other people, those that don't get 'wined and dined' very often, if at all, will appreciate the entire experience (meal, drinks & presentation).

The bottom line: as long as the event is professional and people have a good time while learning about your investment opportunity, your reception will be a success.

When to Host a Reception

Mid-week dates work best for most people. I suggest Tuesday or Wednesday evenings in the spring or fall. Avoid summer meetings, since many people are on vacation. The best starting time is 6:00 PM, and no later than 7:30 PM. I prefer hosting receptions in the evening as opposed to the daytime. The reason for this is that I like it when my attendees can 'make a night of it' by coming to my event to learn about my business. Also, daytime events are tougher for people who have job or family commitments to attend.

The Thing with Investor Receptions…

Most of the time an investor reception is best served as an opportunity to show investors your business, your opportunity and boost your credibility and prestige in their eyes. The reception isn't the best time to collect checks from the investors – and rarely will any write checks to you right there. With this in mind, the reception serves as part one of a two-part process in closing the deal. The second part is getting together with the investor after the reception to get the check or investment commitment.

It may sound strange that you would have an event, spend money, time and energy and, at the end of it, not walk away with money in your hand. This is shortsighted thinking. If you think this way, you also will be disappointed more often than you need to be. Getting private money is a process. It's not a one-stop transaction where you meet someone and get a check on the spot. If you want to be in that business, you should open up a dollar store.

Private money cultivation is a process. When you have a reception and build credibility and excitement as well as present a deal where investors are going to get good returns on their money, you are very close to the "holy grail." All you have to do is follow up properly and you'll get so much private money you won't know what to do with it all (hey, you can always call me!).

Here is a summary of the pros and cons with each meeting format:

Figure 11.1

One-on-One Meeting vs. Reception

	One-on-One	Reception
Connection	More	Less
Excitement	Less	More
Immediacy	More	Less
Investor Value	Less	More

Now that you know the ins and outs of each meeting type, you can set yourself up for success by choosing the format that is right for you and your target investor. Different investors will respond differently in either format. For instance, you may have success with certain investors in a one-on-one environment – they may be the type that are not into all the pomp and circumstance with a reception. There may be other investors who will respond quite favorably to a great reception; your stock will skyrocket in their eyes after you show them a great time.

Whichever route you choose, never lose sight of the main objective of the whole thing: getting private money. If you remember the 5 Private Money Attraction Principles from Part II, you will be putting them on display when you meet with investors. In the next chapter, I'm going to show you how to further put them to work when the most important part of the whole private money process comes up: presenting the deal.

Chapter 12

Presenting the Deal

The meeting is set. Now it's time to present and sell the deal — and I use the term "sell" loosely here. Your ultimate goal is to get the investor to *ask you* if they can invest money with you (although it's quite all right if you ask them, too). Presenting and selling your deal to a private investor represents the culmination of all of your efforts to this point. This chapter will give you a step-by-step plan for presenting the deal to investors for both one-on-one meetings and group presentations.

I have a confession to make: my major motivation for writing this chapter so in depth is that I want you to avoid having to endure some of the long car rides home after failed meetings with investors like I once did. It doesn't feel good to go through all the steps to get in front of a private investor to present your deal and then walk away empty handed. There were many nights of cold sweats when I wasn't sure if I was doing the right thing or not. Stick with the techniques and methods outlined in this chapter and your odds of success will increase by a factor of 10.

The One-on-One Meeting

Preparation is Key

Remember when we discussed *Preparation* as a private money attraction principle? Here is where it really comes into play. To be blunt: it's foolish to go into a meeting with a private investor unprepared. At a minimum, you should spend 2 – 3 hours preparing for your meeting. Know your presentation material forwards and backwards. Carefully rehearse what you will say and how you will say it. Anticipate potential questions, reactions and objections from the investor — and prepare truthful, winning responses. The more prepared you are, the more confident you'll be when presenting the deal, which in turn, inspires the investor's confidence in *you*.

My preferred meeting format (especially when working with new private investors) is one-on-one. The one-on-one format is less formal and more conducive to building a personal relationship with the investor. It's easier to build rapport and trust one-on-one. Potential investors are more open and inquisitive in this environment; asking questions in a room full of people can be intimidating.

When you are getting ready for your meeting, be sure to prepare rebuttals for potential objections your investor may have. Not only will this help you answer the investor's questions, it will also help you craft your message so that you overcome potential objections as you present the deal. Common objections you might hear from private investors include:

> *"This sounds too good to be true."*
>
> *"If it this deal is so great, why hasn't someone else gotten it?"*
>
> *"My attorney/accountant doesn't think this is a good idea."*
>
> *"What happens if the deal goes bad?"*
>
> *"This sounds risky to me..."*

Go into the meeting prepared for objections like these and it won't be long before you're comfortable addressing any concerns an investor may have.

I highly recommend reading books by Zig Ziglar, Tom Hopkins or Jeffrey Gitomer. Reading these great sales trainers will help you tremendously in presenting deals to investors.

Meeting Structure

This is a business meeting, so it's best to adhere to a meeting structure. You should be in control of the meeting from start to finish. When meeting with new investors, I always follow this meeting structure:

- Kickoff
- Present Business/Deal Materials
- Propose Deal
- Ask for Investment
- Investment Commitment
- Conclude Meeting

Your target timeframe for a one-on-one meeting should be one hour — from shaking hands to completing the investment commitment. Certainly, it's acceptable for the meeting to run longer because the investor has questions or because you're working out the fine print of the deal.

―――――――――――――――$$$$ **Resource** $$$$―――――――――――――
Get private investors to say 'yes' the first time.
Sign up for the free 10 week email course at
www.TheBookonPrivateMoney.com.
We cover the private money selling process in Lesson #2
―――――――――――――――――$$$$$$――――――――――――――――――

Kicking off the Meeting

When you kick off the meeting, never plow into the details right away. Don't rush the conversation and don't get pushy. You may be nervous or excited about your deal, but it's okay to make a little small talk. Just stay in control of the conversation. Keep gradually steering the conversation toward your goal. You want to steadily transition the conversation to business matters before presenting.

During your meeting, be mindful of the time. Don't let the small talk and pleasantries drag on for too long. Most investors will be pressed for time, so try to get down to business by the 10-minute mark.

Presenting Materials

The materials you present will play a major role persuading investors to invest money. It's never a good idea to go "naked" into a meeting with a private investor. Always have the details of the investment, your business and any other relevant information along with you. Make sure that you know your materials well and are confident in explaining specific aspects of the deal.

Proposing the Deal

Proposing the deal usually involves referring to an informational document that you've prepared. This "deal sheet" spells out all the important aspects of the deal for the investor, including:

- How much they can invest
- The time frame for the investment
- Proposed return on investment
- Benefits of doing business with you

Throughout the meeting, make sure that you continue to probe for questions or doubts the investor may have. As you go along, ask questions such as: "Does everything look good so far?" Questions like this both propel the conversation forward and alert you if anything you're saying is raising red flags.

As you walk through the deal and address the investor's questions, you should gradually start to weave in questions of proposition, such as: "Does this deal sound like something you'd be interested investing in?" Or: "How would you feel about investing with me?" The answers you get will help you assess the investor's level of interest as they're seeing the details unfold. By asking these questions, you're setting the table for the most important aspect of your meeting with the investor: *asking for the investment.*

Asking for the Investment (or Getting Asked to Invest)
I'm going to let you in on a little secret: The biggest reason real estate investors don't get private money after sitting down with an investor is that they don't *ask for the investment.* Surprised? This may strike you as too simple to be true, but it *is* true. In fact, talk to any good sales coach about the art of selling, and they'll tell you that 'not asking for the order' costs salespeople and companies more sales than they can count. *Never, ever walk away from a meeting with an investor without asking for the investment.*

Here are some of my favorite ways to ask for the investment:

> *"As you can see, this is a great deal. I want to move ahead on this deal with you. Will you move ahead and invest with me?*
> *"From what we've covered, you sound ready to get started. Here's an investment commitment form so we can get things going."*
>
> *"Since it sounds like you're ready, I can set it up so that you can invest right away. Will you be investing with your IRA or other funds?"*

The best two outcomes of your meeting with the investor are: a firm 'yes' or a firm 'no'. You either want a commitment or you want them to say that investing with you is not right for them now. It may sound strange to describe 'No' as a good outcome, but you don't want to waste your time on somebody who's not going to invest with you. There are other fish in the sea. Hopefully at this point you've used some of my targeting and qualifying techniques and you aren't wasting your time on 'tire kickers.' And even if someone says 'No' today, they may still invest money with you in the future. But it's a waste of time to continue trying to persuade someone to do something they aren't ready or able to do. A 'No' allows you to switch your focus to investors who are ready, willing, and able to invest money with you *today.*

Right after you propose a deal and you ask for the investment, the single best thing for you to do is: NOT SPEAK. That's right. Don't say a word. After you ask for the investment, you *must not be the next person to talk.* There is an old adage in business that goes something like this: "The person who talks first after a proposal loses." You must have the discipline to ask for the investment and *stop talking*, or you'll risk unselling the deal.

Other Selling Points

Start Small

To make a new investor feel more comfortable, you may need to start with a smaller investment. If the amount isn't as much as you need to complete the deal, you may need to get creative — find ways to make smaller investment amounts work. Think long-term. Often, it's smarter to take a smaller amount on the first deal and build a relationship that will continue to pay off down the road. Showing the investor a good return on the first deal can lead to larger investment amounts in the future — not to mention glowing referrals. You never know when a $25,000 investor has another $500,000 to invest with you… and several wealthy friends with an extra $500,000 lying around.

Commitment Form

Sometimes you may get a check on the spot (although I do not advise taking in private money without a formal closing or attorney present). The reality is most private investors won't bring their checkbook to the meeting, so you have to use a tangible method to get them committed to investing with you. As the goal of the meeting is for the private investor to commit to investing with you, the most important part of the meeting, then, is getting the investor to complete and sign an investment commitment form.

Make a conscious effort to present the form to the investor as you ask for the investment. Your investment commitment form should contain the basics of the investment, such as amount, interest rate, time frame and the particular property the money is to be invested in. Walk them through each aspect of it. *Never leave the meeting without asking the investor to commit funds!*

Although the commitment form is essentially a 'memorandum of understanding' that has no legally binding effect, the act of signing the form has a psychological impact. The commitment form galvanizes the investor's commitment. It makes the deal *real* in the their mind. Take a look at the following commitment form that I use as an example.

Figure 12.1

Private Money Commitment

A. Private Investor Information

Private Investor (s) Name:_____ _____

Address: _____

City: _____ State: _____ Zip: _____

Date: _____ Approx. Closing Date _____

Investor Signature: _____

B. Project Information

Address: _____

City: _____ State: _____ Zip: _____

County: _____

C. Loan Information

Loan Amount: _____ Term: _____ Interest Rate: _____

Monthly Payment Amt._____ First Payment Date: _____

Type of Loan (circle all that apply): Secured   Unsecured   Interest Only   Balloon

Personal Guarantor Name (if applicable):_____

D. Equity Investment Information

Investment Amount: _____ Term: _____

Investment Type: _____

E. Additional Information/Special Instruction

_____

_____

F. Signatures

_____ _____   _____ _____
Private Investor   Date   Investor/Principal   Date

** ALL FUNDS MUST BE RECEIVED IN CERTIFIED CHECK OR WIRE
AT LEAST 24 HOURS PRIOR TO CLOSING **

After the Investor Commits

Here's a little more "Sales 101" that will be a great help for you in closing private money deals: once the commitment form is completed, steer the conversation away from business as quickly as you can — move on to lighter subject matter. And then conclude the meeting as quickly as possible. Why? You want to avoid further discussion that could cause confusion or lead the investor to have second thoughts and regret the decision. This phenomenon, known as "buyer's remorse," is common, and is especially likely with first time investors, and/or buyers who view the investment as a major purchase.

Some investors are prone to asking additional questions right after they fill out the form, and anything you say at this point could potentially jeopardize the deal. Be careful when answering these post-commitment questions. The best tactic is to refer to your recent conversation (e.g. "like we discussed before…"). Move past those questions quickly and wrap up!

Concluding the Meeting

As you conclude the meeting, be sure to *set the next step*. If the investor has committed funds, agree on a date for the closing. If the investor is using a self-directed IRA, set a deadline to have the materials submitted for funding the IRA. Never leave a meeting without setting the next date for communication. You should always be moving forward — the process is a continuum. Don't leave anything in limbo. Make sure you have the next step planned ahead of time.

Several years ago, I brought in a new private investor for a particular single-family house deal. Everything went well during the meeting and the commitment form was signed. I was moving things ahead toward closing and several days later called the investor to update them on the particulars of the closing time and location. Strangely, my new private investor was nowhere to be found. This was puzzling for me. I called every day for a few days, getting progressively more worried each day. *"Had something happened?"*, I wondered to myself. Boy, this would sure throw a monkey wrench into my deal closing. I called the title company to delay the closing. Just about the time panic set in, I got a call back from my investor. Relief! I thought they had backed out of the deal, so I was pretty inquisitive on the phone with him right away. Soon, I learned what happened.

My private investor had been on vacation. They had no idea of the time frame for our investment, so they just proceeded with their plans without any consideration. I felt blood rush to my face: *"How could they be so cavalier toward investing with me? Don't they know I'm a professional real estate investor?"*

These were the thoughts that were screaming through my head as I listened to what was coming through the other end of the phone. Then, a thought hit me: the whole thing was *my* fault. It was my fault the deal had been delayed and it was my fault the investor had acted so cavalierly toward their investment with me. I had failed to set the next steps and properly prepare my investor for what they needed to do immediately following our meeting.

I quickly snapped my attention back to the conversation and calmly explained to my investor the action steps we needed to take. They happily complied, the deal closed. The investor has been getting a nice steady return on their money ever since. Every time I meet with a private investor, I reflect on this lesson.

If your investor has not committed to investing yet, set a specific date to follow up with them and answer any questions they may still have. Some private investors may not commit immediately because they want to discuss the deal further with their spouse or professional advisor. In this situation, you want to talk to them again *before* they meet with advisors and then schedule a meeting for *after* they talk to advisors. You can also offer to field a conference call with their advisor or spouse as well, to ensure everything goes smoothly.

Wrap up every meeting by shaking the investor's hand, looking him or her in the eye, and thanking them sincerely for taking the time to meet with you.

Where most real estate investors fall short
Post-meeting follow-up is one of the most critical aspects of *getting* that private money in your hands. If the investor committed funds for a deal, call them the next day to re-affirm their decision. Drop them a quick call to say 'thank you' and also send them some form of personal correspondence (letter or stationary card) that contains some affirmative language. People like to be told they've made a wise and prudent decision.

If the investor didn't commit at the meeting but expressed a sincere interest, your post-meeting efforts should be focused on getting the investor to sit down with you again, and commit funds this time. Persistence is very important to success with private money.

Protecting your time
As an entrepreneur, your time is valuable —hey, time *is* money, right? Be protective of your time and invest it wisely. If you ever get the sense that an investor is absolutely not going to place funds with you, don't invest a great deal

of time. Sometimes people run hot and cold on business deals — excited one minute, cold the next. It happens. Don't take it personally. Move on.

Never pursue an investor who firmly tells you they're not interested, or shows you they're not interested by not returning your calls and emails. If you're getting the brush-off, temper your expectations and add this prospect to your marketing pipeline. Send them an email, newsletter or a letter periodically to update them on your business progress or completed transactions. If the prospect seemed at all interested in a deal before, include the numbers from your last deal in the message. This will show them that you're doing business successfully, closing deals without them (see what they're missing), and that you'll have a good opportunity for them in the future.

Presenting to Groups of Investors: The Investor Reception
Many people fear public speaking, but I encourage you to try and conquer that fear — hire a coach if you need to. Otherwise, you're going to miss lucrative opportunities throughout your career. Holding meetings for carefully selected prospective investors allows you to get the most out of your time, to get the most bang for your buck. You might land ten investors for the same two hours of work that you'd have spent in a one-on-one meeting trying to land one investor.

I prefer to call group presentations "Investor Receptions." It's classy and it gives the event a formal and professional feel. To potential investors, "Reception" won't have the ring of "hard-sell" or "get rich quick." There's a certain cachet attached to presentations like this. Investors like to be 'wined and dined' and they like feeling that they're part of something big. A group presentation has this effect on prospective investors.

The biggest challenge of presenting to a group is that it's usually more difficult to get an investor to fully commit funds at the event itself. Usually, your presentation will function as a 'qualifier' for follow up one-on-one meetings, where you can then get the commitment or investment check. The purpose of your group presentation is to gain investors' interest and impress them so they'll be eager to meet with you personally.

So yes, the group presentation can add an extra step to the process — but it can also be a more efficient use of your time — you have the potential to get more private money in less time.

Here's the basic structure I use for investor receptions:
- Setup

- Introduction
- Presentation
- Meal (optional)
- Interest Form
- Post Meeting

Let's explore each aspect in detail…

Setting up the presentation

It's not a good idea to 'fly solo' at your presentation. You'll need someone to help you greet and seat prospects and collect materials such as investment interest forms. You'll also need someone to help you set up and prepare the room. Having someone to assist makes you look more professional — you're not performing as a one-person band.

The group dynamic is different from the one-on-one dynamic, so you'll prepare differently for group presentations. You'll still need to know the deal backward and forward, as you would for a one-on-one meeting, and you still need to be prepared to answer questions and overcome objections. But the group presentation demands more.

Venue, time, and room setup all play a role in whether your investors will leave the event with a positive impression of you. Always confirm arrangements with your venue several days ahead of time. (Imagine what a disaster it would be if twenty people showed up for your reception, only to learn that your banquet room had accidentally been reserved for another event)

Arrive at least 90 minutes before your presentation to ensure that the room is set up properly. Materials you may need include the following:
- Laptop computer
- Projection screen
- Projector
- Extension cords
- Power strips
- Name tags
- PowerPoint Slideshow presentation
- Company materials (set in attractive presentation folders)

- Business cards
- Information about private investing
- Investor handout sheet
- Investment interest form

Don't spend thousands of dollars on equipment. Most of what you will need can be borrowed or rented for few hundred dollars. Have the room set up at least 30 minutes before the scheduled start of the reception. And be aware, you may have some early birds, so you must be prepared *early*.

Introduction

Start the meeting by introducing yourself and thanking everyone for attending. Tell them why they are there and lay out the agenda for the meeting.

Presentation

Visual aids are customary for presentations of this type; for example, a PowerPoint or other slideshow presentation (Keynote for Mac users), which requires a computer and a screen projector. Unless you're an experienced, accomplished speaker, fully confident in your ability to communicate the vital aspects of your opportunity verbally, don't skip this component. The slideshow helps take the pressure off you to remember every single detail in the right sequence.

In addition to PowerPoint presentations, I distribute handouts to each guest — usually a one-page synopsis of why they are there. I never print my overhead slides and distribute them. Why? You want the audience's attention on *you* during the presentation. You don't want to give them any excuse to not pay attention to you. And you don't want them flipping through to the end of the slides. You want to maintain control — you want the presentation to unfold as you designed it to.

I also like to play a short video about my company and the investment opportunity at the beginning of the presentation, then flip through a few slides that detail the investment opportunity. The impact of the video is powerful and it communicates much more than I could, and in a shorter period of time. The video also adds an additional level of professionalism.

When you present, comply with standard public speaking etiquette. Avoid reading the text from your slides. Don't speak too rapidly. For my slideshow, a general benchmark that I shoot for is to speak for 30 seconds per slide. So, for example, if I plan to speak for 15 minutes, I include no more than 30 slides in the presentation. Make sure your slides are clear and concise.

Your text should be no smaller than 20-point font. And don't get cute with fonts. (No Brush Script or Old English) Go for legibility and readability. Don't lose sight of the purpose of your presentation: *To get the investor interested in your deal(s) and to get them to fill out the investment interest form.*

The purpose of your presentation is *not* necessarily to get them to write a check on the spot. Some investors may pounce on the opportunity right away, but the structure of your presentation should be to stimulate intense interest, entice the investor to crave more information about investing with you, and to provide you with the information you need to have a productive one-on-one meeting with them.

Shape your presentation in general terms — avoid going into too much detail, which can overwhelm people and leave them with that "glassed over" look in their eyes. The more detail you provide during your presentation, the more explaining you'll have to do, and the more likely it is that your audience's attention will drift off — the presentation will lose focus. Keep the audience engaged throughout the presentation. Give them bits of information that make them curious and compelled to hear more.

Interest Form

Make sure every prospective investor fills out an interest form and that you collect it before they leave. This is important. The interest form is the most critical component of the group meeting. It gives you a connection to your investor for a follow-up dialogue, and will give you an idea of how much money they have to invest and where the funds are coming from. Make sure every attendee fills out an interest form before they leave. It's also a good idea to give each attendee a free gift that, of course, has your company name or logo on it. Never let your investors leave empty-handed.

What Happens After the Reception?

The most important part of an investor group presentation is what you do *after* the meeting. *The number one mistake real estate investors make is failing to follow up properly with meeting attendees.* And it's one of the most expensive mistakes you can make.

First, go through the interest forms you collected. Call each investor personally to thank him or her for attending the reception and schedule an appointment for a sit-down meeting. Also, send a 'Thank You' card to each person. Be sure the card includes your contact information. The card, coupled with the personal phone call, will ensure they don't forget you, and that your investment opportunity never strays too far from their thoughts.

It's best to contact each investor within two days of the meeting. Interest tends to wane over time, so you want to strike while the iron is hot. Get that one-on-one meeting scheduled while your presentation and opportunity are still fresh in their minds.

Turn on the Pipeline of Private Money
Now that you know exactly how to present your deals to investors in both one-on-one and group situations, you can really create a pipeline of private money for yourself. You have the tools to close any private money deal at any time. As long as you adhere to the private money attraction principles and take consistent action, you'll never walk away empty-handed.

The process of presenting deals to potential investors can be exciting. One of the very best parts of being a real estate investor is that you have opportunities, again and again, to help create wealth for other people. Hold that thought in your mind as you present deals to potential investors. Be yourself, be prepared, demonstrate *opportunity*. The private money will pour in.

Chapter 13

What Rate of Return Should You Pay?

One of the most difficult questions you'll have to grapple with is: "What return should I pay my investor?" If you have this question, you're certainly not alone. Companies large and small wrestle with this question every day. Large global companies spend days working out their dividend policy. Start-up businesses pore over the numbers with their venture capitalists to decide what the return on investment (ROI) should be.

This perpetual debate about ROI is the result of an inherent conflict of interest that arises when you're dealing with investor money: You want to pay the lowest return possible in order to maximize your profits while still getting the money you need, and private investors want to receive the highest return possible for the dollars they invest. This struggle will always be part of capitalism and, thus, part of funding real estate deals. You have to be practical and take a long-term view.

Like many things in business, the rate of return you give your investor is subject to negotiation. I've found the best strategy is to propose a deal that has a rate of return built into it. This projected return represents my 'first offer' to the investor, and they often take it. The first rate of return I propose in a deal is often not the *highest* I would be wiling to pay, but it's obviously a return I'd be happy with, and it serves as a good starting point.

And here's a little secret: Most investors won't want to haggle over the rate of return. As long as your proposal makes sense and is believable, they won't feel the need for any complex back-and-forth negotiation.

Avoid any kind of hostile exchange with your investor. If their rate of return demands are unreasonable, or if they want too large of a percentage of a deal, just back off and make sure you're both on the same page. When investors are being unreasonable, it's helpful to go back through the deal and demonstrate the value you're providing, compared to the alternative investments available.

Investors usually view rates of return on investment in relative terms. If bank CD rates are yielding 3% and government bonds are yielding 5%, a 9%

return from a secured real estate investment looks very attractive. However, if bank CD rates were 8%, then a 9% return on a real estate investment isn't very appealing. The investor may think: "Why take any extra risk when I only have to take 1% less *and* it's FDIC insured?"

Stock market performance can affect an investor's mindset as well. If stocks are returning gains of 10% to 15% or more per year, as they were throughout much of the 1980s and 1990's, returns on private money real estate investments that don't compare favorably will be less attractive.

Let's go through an example to demonstrate: Say you were going to buy, fix and flip a single family home. If you buy the house for $100,000 and it needs $25,000 in repairs, you would want to get about $130,000 in private money. Why the extra $5,000? Because you want to make sure you have enough for contingencies — unexpected costs. You don't want to go back to the investor for more money later. It's more time, hassle and paperwork for everyone and you can pre-empt it from the start.

Now, on this type of deal, I might start by offering an investor a private money loan at 10% simple interest per year. If the loan is secured by a first lien, the investor would be getting a nice margin of safety on their investment and a healthy return. If I was going to bring in two investors, the investor that brought the majority of the cash would get first lien and the investor with the subordinate lien would get a slightly higher interest rate, perhaps a 12% return in this case.

When the house sells, I would pay back the lender their interest, prorated based on the holding time. For example, if I borrowed the entire $130,000 in private money on a first mortgage at 10% annual interest and I held the property for 3 months, I would pay the lender $3,250 in interest.

Figure 13.1

Private Loan Interest Breakdown	
Loan amount	$130,000
Loan Term	3 Months
Interest Rate	10%
Monthly Interest	$1,083
Interest Paid	$3,250
Total Cost of Funds	$3,250

Remember, your private investors will earn interest according to the time period in which their funds are invested. Some real estate investors erroneously believe the lender is owed a total of 10% on their money regardless of time invested. However, the rate of return you are providing should always be an *annualized* rate of return.

Another way I might structure a private money deal would be to bring the investor in as an equity partner. They would commit their funds for a period of time and receive a share of the profits and cash flows from the deals we would do together with their money. For instance, let's say I was going to buy a house, renovate it and then sell it on a lease-option. With a "rent-to-own" buyer in the house, I would get $1,200 per month in rent, resulting approximately $700 per month operating cash flow (before debt service) as well as receive a $5,000 option fee (which would be credited against their final purchase price when the house sold). For the purposes of our example here, the sale price is $175,000.

Using the same numbers as we did earlier before for purchase price and rehab, if I were to buy the same property for $125,000 and then sell it on a lease-option, I might bring in an equity partner for the private money and split the profits 50/50. The equity partner would bring the $130,000 in cash and I would agree to handle everything else (renovation, management, selling).

You might be wondering why I would use an equity partner versus a lender for this type of deal. The reason is: with a private *lender* funding the entire purchase and rehab, the $1,000+ per month loan payment would eliminate my cash flow (when operating expenses are considered). Negative cash flow is absolute "no-no". I have seen real estate investors have their businesses completely wiped out by just a few negative cash flow properties.

With an equity investor in the deal, there is no minimum loan payment; instead there is a profit sharing arrangement on the sale proceeds and cash flow. With this deal structure, the investor would be making approximately $350 per month in cash flow ($750 per month/2). This is a cash return of $4,200 per year. If you do the math, you'd see that they would only be getting a 2% return on their $130,000 investment. But, don't forget that they also get *50% of the proceeds on sale*. Since I'm going to be selling for a $50,000 profit in two years, the private investor would receive $25,000 in profit sharing on the sale.

In our example, if we add up what the private equity investor will receive both in cash flow and sale profit sharing, they would receive $8,400 (two years of cash flow) and $25,000 on the sale, for a total cash return of $33,400. Their $33,400 return on investment is equivalent to approximately 13% per year return on their money. And, don't forget the biggest chunk of their profit is taxed at long-term capital gain rates, which are lower than tax rates on ordinary income.

I've had great success paying rates of 8% to 12% per year for private money loans and 10% to 15% annual rates of return to my equity investors. There are many deals where the returns for equity investing *far* exceed these rates, but it's always better to under-promise and over-deliver. And being more conservative with your profit projections helps manage investor expectations. Sometimes the returns on one deal are abnormally good and you don't want the investor to be upset with you if they don't get that same return on *every* deal.

For example, I once had a lender who was receiving 10% simple interest paid monthly; the house he was lending on was sold. We then offered him an opportunity to invest as an equity partner in a deal for a 15% return. This deal cashed out after roughly five months and the investor was happy. He wanted to keep his funds invested with us, but the next deal we had was for a loan on a house at 10% simple interest again. He was upset about having to "settle for" a return of 10% — that fatter 15% return had spoiled him. It took a lot of effort to make him feel good about accepting 10% interest again. The moral of the story is: be cautious about conditioning your investors to expect returns that are higher than you're comfortable consistently paying.

One of the hallmarks of investing with you should be consistency and reliability. Your investors can count on their check arriving on time. You can ease their fears about the volatilities of the stock market. When you set up your private money deals the right way, you'll be laying the groundwork for reliable returns that will keep your investors coming back to you again and again with more funds to invest.

When you work with a new investor, it's easy to do or say whatever it takes to get the money. But whatever you do, don't promise returns that are too high to be feasible. If you propose a return that's extraordinarily high, it will affect your credibility. Your investor will simply decide that it's 'too good to be true.' If you promise a higher return than your deal can justify financially, you're setting yourself up for trouble. It's okay to give up some of your profits to private investors, but you should still ensure the deal is worth your time. This is how you build a big business.

In the end, the best way to align your interests with those of your investor is to construct that win-win — you earn a good profit by helping them get good returns on their money.

Chapter 14

Closing the Deal

You're running down the field with the end zone in sight... you've dodged or hurdled every obstacle, weaved your way through every objection ... crossing the 10-yard line ... "Yes, please let me write you a check!" the private investor is saying... the 8-yard line...6... 4 — *three feet from a touchdown!* and —
you fumble the ball on the 2-yard line! The private investor bails. The deal goes south. Your profits are lost.

What happened? You didn't know what to do after the investor said 'yes.' *You didn't know how to close the deal.*

The closing strategies you're about to learn in this chapter will assure that you never fumble the ball on your way to the end zone. There are plenty of ways to jeopardize a private money deal. You need to avoid some landmines. When the deal goes off the rails after the private investor was ready to write the check, it's usually not due to one big mistake, but a combination of mistakes. In a minute, we'll talk about how hit 'paydirt,' but let's get a few housekeeping rules out of the way.

Closing Agents

Every private money deal should be closed using a third party — a title company or an attorney. Avoid taking money directly from your private investor without having a qualified closing agent present to help facilitate the movement of those funds. Trust me on this one. Using a closing agent greatly reduces the odds of future problems. Having a reputable third party to facilitate the paperwork (including notarizing documents performing the transfer of funds, recording documents at the county register of deeds, etc.) will also put your investor at ease.

The presence of a closing agent makes the deal feel "official" to your investor and will inspire more confidence in you. You must be a professional who fulfills his/her commitment completely, including 'dotting the i's and crossing the t's'.

Taking funds from a private investor with no closing agent present can expose you to deal-breaker issues or even potential legal problems. One problem, for example, might be a 'he said, she said' conflict. The investor could claim that you offered them specific terms that you didn't really offer them, or there could be issues with the investment amount and timing. Certainly, this won't always be the case, and some investors will be easier to deal with than others. Just be aware that we live in a litigious society, and it's always wise to take small, low-cost measures to protect yourself (and your investor).

Closing Venue

Always strive to have your private money closing take place at a title company or attorney's office. When you're dealing with a private money loan, this often happens in the natural course of the transaction, anyway. However, there are many times when you will receive the funding from the investor before the closing date. When that happens, simply setting up an escrow account at the title company or with the closing attorney provides a safe holding tank for the funds until closing.

Deal Closing Land mines

Step on any one of these land mines and your deal can skid sideways in a hurry…

Improper Follow-up

If you've ever been nagged by second thoughts after purchasing a big ticket item, such as a new car or a house, you understand the powerful psychology of "buyer's remorse." Your private investor may begin to have second thoughts about his decision to invest with you, or fear that he rushed to a decision too quickly, that he has made a bad investment.

You may need an antidote for buyer's remorse. You can neutralize it by taking immediate steps to reassure your private investor that he made the right decision in investing with you. Sometimes, the simplest actions are enough to do the trick. First, after your private investor says 'yes,' immediately reassure them that they are making the right decision. Next, send them a gift — the very next day. A basket of muffins, a bottle of wine, a gift certificate to a fancy restaurant. Be creative, but be appropriate. Accompanying the gift should be a card that thanks them for doing business with you, and reiterates your optimism about a mutually beneficial future together. You don't have to be fancy, and you certainly don't want to be sappy. Just be genuine.

Never let your investor think — even for a second — that doing business with you is anything less than an absolute joy. You will never regret treating your investors like gold.

Lack of Definitive Action

Once you get a commitment from a private investor, you must immediately lay out the next steps for them. It's okay to tell the investor what to do. You're not being bossy. You're in charge. Your investor will *expect* you to take a leadership role and shepherd the deal to completion. Investors need clear direction — especially if they haven't been involved in a similar transaction before.

---$$$$ Resource $$$$---
You'll benefit greatly by reading *Low Profile Selling* by Tom Hopkins and *Secrets of Closing the Sale* by Zig Ziglar
---$$$$$$---

Miscommunication

It's easy, in the heat of presenting and persuading, to brush past a little detail that will be important to the closing process. But many private money deals blow up because the real estate investor failed to communicate a particular aspect of the deal to the private investor.

For instance, I remember a deal in which I was selling a two-house package. The investor who was purchasing the properties from me was using two private investors; one for each property. Everything looked good, right up until two days before closing; I received a phone call on a Friday afternoon, and it wasn't good news…

My buyer proceeded to tell me that he had to back out of the deal because his private investor couldn't get the funds together by the Tuesday closing date we had set. When I pressed for details, he told me his private investor thought that he had access to his funds, then later found out there was a *6-month delay* before he could access the funds from his retirement account — six months! We didn't have six months, of course. The deal was blown.

Scheduling Problems/Conflicts

We all have busy lives, your private investors included. A clear timeframe is one of the most important aspects of closing that you must outline for your investor once they've agreed to invest with you. Make sure they have time to put their affairs in order. This can be particularly important if the investor has estate, tax, or other needs that must be taken into consideration when they move money from point A to point B. Be considerate of this and open a dialogue about it right away to ensure there are no last-minute surprises.

Once you set a closing date, stick to it. Communicate with your private investors. Send them a reminder as the closing date approaches.

If it seems at all possible that there might be a delay — either on your end or your investor's — be proactive. Re-schedule the closing so that everyone can be completely ready. Don't reschedule for frivolous reasons, but if a legitimate reason for rescheduling arises, do it. Don't blow your deal.

How to REALLY Mess Up the Deal
Now, there are a handful of tactics that are guaranteed to blast a deal to smithereens. These aren't just little boo-boo's — these are deal killers. Which means you must avoid them at all costs.

Changing the Game
Once you have an agreement with a private investor, verbal or otherwise, you'd better stick to it. The most old-fashioned adage in business, 'Your word is your bond,' may be out of style in today's business environment, but it should never go out of style for *your* business. Never, and I mean *never* change the terms of a deal without notifying your private investor.

What counts as changing the game? Examples include: moving their money into deals that were not discussed, paying them a different rate of return than was agreed upon, or distributing funds to them on a schedule they were unaware of or did not agree to. If you need to make changes, simply talk to your investor. Usually, they'll understand, and they'll appreciate your honesty. Business situations change, and often, the deal must change with it. Just communicate, and keep everything above-board. If you lose integrity in the eyes of the investor, you have nothing. No deal. No profits. No reputation.

Disappearing
Avoid being incommunicado in the immediate period after the private money deal is committed or funded. Everyone needs to take a vacation now and then, but if you're going out of town right after you do a private money deal, be sure to stay accessible. Your private investor may need to contact you about something important. Plus, it really makes investors nervous if the person they just invested money with is suddenly unreachable. They'll tend to think the worst (especially these days), even if their fears are unfounded.

Avoiding Your Private Investors Advisors
Be prepared: Often, your private investors' professional advisors are going to be involved in the deal. It may be an attorney reviewing investment documents, a CPA advising them on the tax impact of their investment with you, or a financial planner who's angry that your investor is diverting money from their stock market account to your deal. Whoever the advisor or whatever the case,

make sure that you are professional and courteous when dealing with your private investors' advisors.

Some real estate investors fear their private investor's advisors will be deal killers so they avoid them like the plague. Don't make this mistake! Your private investor will sense it and wonder why you're avoiding his advisors. If you won't take a quick phone call from his attorney to answer a simple question about a promissory note, your investor will wonder if investing with you is such a good idea. Remember to always put yourself in the investor's shoes.

It's easy to overlook a couple of details when you're closing a private money deal. But overlook too many and you can wave bye-bye to all the hard work you've put in to land the investors. The bigger the deal and the bigger the investment, the higher the stakes...

Don't be nervous. Be *conscientious*. Be proactive. You can mitigate potential problems by having competent, experienced advisors in *your* corner. A strong power team — attorney, CPA, mentor — can help guide you through any questions along the way. Retain advisors you can trust and use them. Don't hesitate to ask questions of your advisors and service providers — and demand the answers you need to get the deal done. Lock every deal down airtight and closing day will be a breeze.

PART V

Other Important Things With Private Money

Congratulations! At this point you can give yourself a pat on the back. You've made it through the basics and you now know exactly what you need to do to successfully bring in private money. You deserve a lot of credit and many of your real estate investing colleagues are going to be eating your dust soon.

While we have covered the basics with private money, there are a few more important things to know. In fact, there's *a lot* more you need to know, but we're going to take it one thing at a time. The important thing for you to do right now is *focus on taking action*. It's never too early to begin marketing for investors and preparing for deals to present.

For me, one of the most difficult things in driving private money into my business was getting out of the starting blocks. It was difficult at first, mostly because I didn't know where to start. I didn't have a good road map in front of me, or good resources – like this book – to guide me. Fortunately, you have some great resources at your disposal right here and you should take full advantage.

Some of the intricacies with private money, such as taxes and securities laws, are going to require you to put your thinking cap on a little bit. It really is important stuff, and I would be remiss if I didn't cover these important aspects.

So, let's keep rolling…

Chapter 15

What <u>Not</u> To Do

The preceding chapters in this book have armed you with the knowledge you need and the specific techniques you can employ to raise private investment capital in a *very short* period of time. The approach we have taken so far has been focused on showing you what you need *to do* in order to attract private money, meet investors and propose and close deals. But, equally as important as what *to do* with getting private money is knowing what *not to do*.

I have found over the years that a lot of investors can get stuck in 'no-man's land' when they first start out. This getting stuck in no-mans land is due in large part to not knowing specific mistakes to avoid.

The private money process can be divided into two parts: *before* the investment commitment and *after* the investment commitment. The remainder of this chapter is dedicated to giving you some specific examples of what NOT to do with private investors both before they invest with you *and* after they have committed those funds.

There Are Only Two Sure Things in Life…
It has been said that there are only two sure things in life: death and taxes Investing with you could be a good investment decision for the private investor, but when you start going overboard and promising returns up and down and throwing the word 'guarantee' around, little red flags raise in the investor's mind.

Overusing the word "guarantee" is a big mistake. The only time you should ever use this word when dealing with private money is with regard to a personal guarantee for a private money loan. One of the absolute worst things you can do is to rush into guaranteeing a certain rate of return on an investment.

The only investments that are truly guaranteed are those that are backed by the full faith and credit of the United States Government. Most private investors will know this as well, so alarm bells in their heads will go off if you go overboard promising and guaranteeing them returns.

Leave the Slips to Tricky Dick & Slick Willie
Politicians are extremely good at appearing as if they are giving answers to questions when they are actually just spitting out non-answers. Despite the mistrust of politicians by the general public, a lot of business people like to try and emulate them by giving evasive or incomplete answers to private investor questions.

If an investor asks you a question and you try to duck it, give an incomplete answer or even make up an answer, you are setting yourself up for trouble. The best thing to do is to take their questions head-on. You will no doubt face tough questions like: "How do I know that you won't steal my money?" When you get these questions, remember: *YOU*, the real estate investor, the one asking for the money are the *expert*. If you prepare using the guidelines I gave you earlier, none of this should be a problem for you.

Another thing: if you 'punt' questions too often, saying things like "I'll have to check on that", it will start to undermine the investor's confidence in you. Make sure you are comfortable with *at least* the basics when you sit down with an investor, otherwise it may be a waste of a meeting.

Here are a few surefire ways to blow up a private money deal or screw things up with your investor *after they commit* to investing with you:

Don't Overkill It
Once the investor says 'yes' to investing with you, STOP trying to sell them on the investment. You don't need to keep the charm on full blast the whole way through. In fact, it often works to your detriment if you keep re-iterating all the wonderful reasons to invest with you *after* they have already agreed to invest.

At some point (count on it being soon after they commit to investing funds or write you a check) the investor will be in a delicate mental place (at least most investors will be). Think of the last time you made a major purchase, like a car or home. How did you feel immediately after you signed your name and bought it? Did you feel a little uneasy, unsure of yourself maybe? This is completely natural and happens in most people after big purchase decisions. Since your investor just parted with $50,000, $100,000, or more, to invest with you, it qualifies as the same type of large decision as a car or home purchase.

You should focus on re-assuring the investor in subtle ways that they made the right choice, not continue to browbeat them with all of the bells and whistles of the deal. They've already made the decision to invest with you. You've won them over. Your next step to winning them over again is not going to be with words, it is going to be with actions.

Immediately after someone agrees to invest with me, I look them in the eye and tell them they are making a good decision. It takes about five seconds to accomplish and works wonders for making them feel better about their decision. Soon after, I like to change the subject to ease any tension or worry. I'll talk about an upcoming holiday or season, share a funny story, or discuss an interesting local news story. My goal is to keep the conversation light and off the subject of business.

Know Thy Details, Grasshopper
As you've probably noticed throughout this book, one of my big secrets to getting private money is to continually put yourself in the investor's shoes. In any investment (stock, bond, real estate or other) money moves from one place to another through intermediaries (banks, title companies, brokerages) and there is almost always paperwork involved. Attention to detail throughout the private money investment process — from the investor to you — is important.

If you are not at least familiar with the details for how the money will move from A to B to C, your private investor will be leery. Almost every investor will ask you what they need to do or what is involved in the investment process. Nobody likes the thought of their money being tied up in limbo somewhere and they certainly don't like the thought that you aren't well-versed with the process. Make sure you understand each step of the private money closing process. Don't hesitate to involve your attorney in any matters with private money. Even though it may cost you a little extra, it wil save you a lot of headaches (and wallet-aches).

Dazed and Confused
Most of your private investors won't be sophisticated professional investors. They may have a little experience in managing their own savings and investments, but for the most part they are going to look to you for critical pieces of information on the investment. This is a big danger zone: avoid confusing your investors at all costs. Confusion leads to indecision, which leads to no investment with you.

After you learn the investor's needs and preferences, propose the deal in the simplest way possible. Break it down into discrete steps ("step 1, step 2…"). Avoid using confusing terms and industry jargon.

For example, for a private mortgage loan, try breaking it down like this:

    Step 1: Investment commitment/agreement
    Step 2: Locate investment
    Step 3: Funding procurement and closing

Tell the investor you will be handling all the details, so they don't feel like they have to take unnecessary time out of their lives. People are used to some level of convenience with their investments (for the most part at least). At big financial services companies, most of the paperwork processing is handled out of site of the client. With a private money deal, you must handle some of these administrative functions, such as making sure the title company or attorney has the proper paperwork, obtaining signatures, etc.

One of my first private investors was a very 'hands-off' type of person. They were very intimidated by any type of paperwork or forms having to do with investments. This was problematic, because some amount of paperwork is necessary in every deal. I wanted to keep everything above board, so one day I sat down with the investor and explained to them the documents they had to sign and why they were necessary.

Suddenly, like magic, the investor's entire outlook changed and there were no more problems with paperwork. What I learned from this was that people are very leery of signing forms and documents they don't know or don't understand. Simply explaining the rationale behind signing a direction of investment or an instruction letter for a title company or a limited partnership agreement can go a long way toward alleviating any concerns your private investors may have.

Don't Shoot Yourself in the Foot...

Since private money is such a critical part of your business and you are going to be putting some time in up front, it's important you don't shoot yourself in the foot. Essentially, this chapter amounts to: a 'How to not shoot yourself in the foot' guide. I encourage you to read and re-read this chapter often, especially as you begin to meet with and propose deals to investors. You'll be amazed at how many situations come up where it is easy to go down the wrong path. Stick with my guidelines and you'll sleep a lot easier at night – and so will your investors.

Chapter 16

Private Money Goldmine - Self-Directed IRAs

One of the most important tools you can use to bring in loads of private money is: self-directed retirement accounts. I can't think of any other single tool that has resulted in more private money for me. There are various types of self-directed retirement accounts available, but for the sake of simplicity, we're just going to throw them all under the umbrella of 'self-directed IRAs.' No matter what you call them, they will be one of the best weapons in your arsenal to get private money.

Here's an interesting experiment: ask the next person you talk to if they knew they could invest in real estate with their IRA. My guess is at least 9 out of 10 people are completely unaware they can do this. Most of the general investing public is conditioned to believe they can only invest in IRAs with mutual funds, stocks, bonds, annuities, or other forms of 'traditional' assets.

This brainwashing done by the marketers on Wall Street can actually work to *your advantage*. Because most people are unaware they can invest in real estate with their IRAs, they will be very open to learning about it from *you*. I've gotten huge sums of private money from simply putting myself in the position of educating the private investor about self-directed IRAs; my company was then the logical choice to invest in for them.

What Exactly is a Self-Directed IRA?
A self-directed IRA is simply an Individual Retirement Account in which the owner of the account makes the investment decisions. Self-directed IRAs are not typically limited to a select group of assets, such stocks or mutual funds. Tax regulations require either a custodian or qualified trustee hold the assets on behalf of the IRA owner. The custodian keeps track of all the tax related information and fulfills reporting and recordkeeping requirements.

Self-directed IRAs are just like other IRAs: the contribution amounts, tax treatment and reporting requirements to the IRS are all the same. There are self-directed traditional and ROTH IRAs, 401(k)s, SIMPLE IRAs and SEP IRAs. Anyone from a small individual investor to a company with hundreds of employees can utilize self-directed retirement accounts.

So why don't more people know about self-directed IRAs? Is there some kind of conspiracy going on? Probably not. I do think the financial services industry profits a lot more by *not* offering self-directed IRAs or by restricting what you can invest in with their version of a self-directed (usually not real estate).

Getting Started With Self-Directed IRAs

Getting started with a Self-Directed IRA is just as easy as opening up any other kind of investment account. You fill out the account application paperwork, pay a small fee, and the account is open.

In order to open an account, though, you first have to find a company through which your private investor will manage their IRA. There are actually quite a few of them out there, but it's important that you use a reputable IRA custodian that is easy to work with. The two primary self-directed IRA companies I have used the most and recommend to my private investors are Equity Trust Company and The Entrust Group.

―――――――――――――$$$$ Resource $$$$―――――――――――――
Equity Trust Company - www.TrustETC.com
The Entrust Group - www.TheEntrustGroup.com
―――――――――――――$$$$$$―――――――――――――

Opening an account with these companies is quite simple: just download an application form off of their website or use the online application setup process. It should not take more than an hour or so. The most important decisions to be made at this point are what type of self-directed retirement account your investor will be opening. Often, the account type will be the same as the currently have (ROTH, Traditional, etc.).

Your next step is to have the investor fund the IRA. This can be a bit tricky. If your investor is funding their IRA with a one-time contribution, then it's pretty easy – they simply send a check into the custodian. However, the most likely scenario is that your investor is going to be moving assets from another IRA to their self-directed. In the investment world, this is called a *transfer*.

There are two basic types of transfers: a transfer of cash or a transfer of securities. Your investor can either instruct their current custodian to sell a given amount of assets (called securities - stocks, bonds, mutual funds) and then send the cash proceeds over to the self-directed custodian or they can instruct the current custodian to send the securities over to the self-directed custodian. The self-directed custodian would then have to execute the trades to convert the securities into the cash that will be invested with you.

Here is an example to better illustrate:

> Let's say your private Investor has $500,000 invested in mutual funds in their IRA account at ABC Investments, Inc. They agree to invest $100,000 with you through a self-directed IRA, using Friendly IRA Co. as the custodian.
>
> *With a transfer of cash*: the private investor would instruct ABC Investments, Inc to sell $100,000 worth of mutual fund shares. The cash from the proceeds of this sale would then be transferred to Friendly IRA Co. Then, from Friendly IRA Co, the investment would go into the deal with you.
>
> *With a transfer of securities:* $100,000 of mutual fund shares would be sent from ABC Investments, Inc to Friendly IRA Co. Friendly IRA Co. would then sell the mutual fund shares. The cash proceeds from this sale would then be available for investment in the deal with you.

Keep in mind there are often costs associated with selling securities and transferring assets, such as commissions, wire fees or processing fees. Make sure that you find out what these will be ahead of time.

Once the self-directed IRA is funded, the next step is to get the money into your investment deal. This is done with a *direction of investment* form, or DOI. The DOI instructs the custodian where to send the money and what type of investment it will be (promissory note, equity ownership, etc.). You have to be very careful about how you fill out the DOI paperwork. The compliance departments at the IRA custodians will scrutinize every detail – so make sure you ask any question of them that will help you fill the paperwork out correctly the first time.

One of the first times I did a big private placement (equity investment) with one of my investor's self-directed IRAs, I ran into a snag because of a discrepancy on the DOI paperwork. The issue eventually got kicked up to the head of the compliance department at the IRA custodian and, after hours and hours of back and forth, we finally got everything squared away. No sweat, right? Here was the rub: I had to push back several deal closings and also had to postpone the return on investment my private investor was going be receiving. The situation could have easily made the investor mad or gave them pause. None of those are good things.

This brings me to another important point: your private investor is not making anything on their money if it is sitting in cash at the IRA custodian. These funds must be invested in a deal with you or you risk having an unhappy investor. I know that some real estate investors will start paying returns to the private investor as soon as the funds are moved from their old IRA, but I do not advise this. You should always be paying your private investors their returns out of the cash flow of a project, not out of your pocket. The latter is a fast way to get yourself in a heap of trouble.

OK, Great…But How Much Does It Cost?
The fees for opening, funding and maintaining a self-directed IRA are quite reasonable. On average, plan on spending less than .5% of the total asset value of the account each year in maintenance fees. You can generally open an account for less than $100 (not including wire fees and other fees that may apply). All told, self-directed IRAs are extremely cost effective.

Self-Directed IRA POWER
Since most of the people you will talk to about private money won't know they can invest in real estate with their IRA, you have the elements of surprise and intrigue working for you. You are offering something new and different, which always bodes well for getting someone's rapt attention. You can also take on the role of educator, which further establishes your credibility with the private investor.

Of course, the most powerful aspect of self-directed IRAs is that your private investor can compound their wealth by investing with you and enjoy tax deferred or tax free treatment of those gains. Tax deferred gains are very beneficial, because your investor can essentially use money owed to the government to *grow their nest egg*. Take a look at the following graph, which shows the power of deferring taxes to compound wealth:

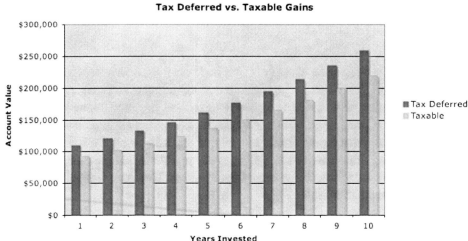

Figure 16.1 shows compound annual gains on an invested amount of $100,000 at 10% per year for 10 years. The taxable investment is assumed to be taxed at an ordinary income tax rate of 15%.

Demonstrating the power of tax-deferred gains, the investor's account balance grows to be worth over $38,000 *more* than the taxable account after just 10 years, even though the rate of return is the same. This huge difference is due to deferring the income taxes owed each year. Each year the amount of money that is technically owed to the IRS is being compounded upon. The less money paid out in taxes, the bigger the balance left to grow on for the next year, and so on.

Now, if you're reading between the lines here, you can feel good knowing you're using Uncle Sam's nickel to help your private investor grow wealthier while pumping more money into your bank account as well. Keep in mind that anything withdrawn from a tax-deferred account is taxed at ordinary income when it is taken out, but your investors will still have a bigger pile of money to draw on than they otherwise would have. It's a pretty sweet deal if you take advantage of it.

One other huge bonus with current tax laws is that, through a self-directed ROTH IRA, the gains made are *tax-free* if the account has been open at least 5 years and the investor is over the age of 59 ½. Essentially, this means that your private investor could build a tremendous amount of tax-free wealth by investing in your business with a self-directed ROTH IRA.

As soon as I un-corked this benefit for potential private investors I was talking to, it gave me a huge boost in getting them to invest with me. Sometimes you just need that little extra push, that small added benefit (tax free wealth is a big one) and it pushes the investor over to your side and they are eager to invest with you.

Things To Think About With Self-Directed IRAs

Once your private investor agrees to place funds with you through an IRA, there are some factors you must consider to make sure everything goes off without a hitch.

IRA Rules

The IRS is *very* strict about what can be deemed a taxable event with regard to IRAs. This is why it is always better to transfer money from one IRA to the self-directed IRA versus a rollover (where the old IRA company cuts a check to the investor and there is a 60 day window to get the money re-invested). In my experience, transfers are much easier than rollovers from an administrative standpoint.

Additionally, special care must be taken that the private investor not perform any compensation based work on the property(s) in which their IRA is invested. This could be deemed a taxable distribution from the IRA. Also, the investor may not personally receive a distribution from the profits of the deal, any distributions generated by projects or deals funded with the investors IRA must be paid back to the IRA.

Unfriendliness of Financial Service Companies

When your private investor goes to move money from their IRA or 401(k) into a self-directed IRA to invest with you, don't expect this to be warmly received by the company where their money currently is held. I have yet to meet a financial services company or a retirement planner that is happy when their client tells them they are pulling a substantial sum of money out to put into a self-directed IRA. Most of the time, these financial service companies and their associates are compensated based on the amount of money invested and/or the products the client purchases.

With this being the case, there may be some friction when your private investor goes to pull money out of their account. I have even seen financial planners get downright hostile toward the client, telling them they are going to lose money in 'that real estate deal' and even worse! Do your private investor a favor and prepare them for this circumstance. It's nothing to be overly concerned about, but it always helps to lay the right groundwork.

Timing

Be careful in matching the time frame in which you are placing the private investors funds with how long the self-directed IRA process will take. On more than one occasion things have gotten pretty dicey for me when I was first starting with private money and self-directed IRAs because the IRA account had not funded the investment and my deal was ready to close. Avoid this problem by managing the closing date with the IRA set up and direction of investment process.

If the investor is making a one-time contribution upon opening their self-directed IRA, it should take no more than 5-7 business days to have the funds ready to place in your deal. However, when your private investor is transferring money from their old IRA company to a self-directed, the process could take 14-20 business days. It all depends on the amount of money being moved, the type of assets being sold or transferred and the overall speed with which the IRA company works (sometimes at a snail's pace).

Go Forth and Self-Direct

If there were a way for me to encourage you to be more aggressive in using self-directed IRAs to get private money, I would employ it. I guarantee if you use these tools the right way that you will get private investors. There are so many benefits to investing in real estate with an IRA that you should have to beat investors off with a stick.

As you move forward and employ this strategy, it will be very beneficial for you to know some of the ins and outs with how self-directed IRAs work. Spend some time finding an IRA custodian (start with the two companies mentioned earlier) and go through their website. Download some materials and learn more about how the investment process works. All of this will help you better communicate with your private investors and will arm you with more knowledge to close big private money deals.

Chapter 17

Taxes

Yes, this chapter will explore a subject you'd probably prefer not to think about. However, as a thriving real estate investor, the taxman is going be part of your life — count on it. Uncle Sam always gets his cut, and if you don't give it to him voluntarily, sooner or later, he'll force you to give it up.

Taxes are a thorn in every business owner's side. It often feels that not only do we have to work hard to make our money, but we have to work hard to keep it as well. The trick is to minimize Uncle Sam's cut. Fortunately, tax breaks for real estate investments are more plentiful than in practically any other investment sector. In real estate, we get deductions and credits that can help minimize our tax burden such as "pass-through losses," "depreciation" and "1031 exchanges."

The tax aspect of private money is often overlooked. It's not hard to understand why: navigating your way through the complex U.S. tax code can be daunting. As a 'user' of private money, you incur certain responsibilities, which we'll discuss in this chapter.

But it's not all bad news…

How to Leverage the Tax Code to Get Private Money
Sound crazy? It's true! Think about it: if *you* can receive tax benefits from real estate investing, your private investors can as well. And here's the kicker: Private money tax benefits can provide you with persuasive ammunition when proposing deals to potential investors. In other words, understanding a little bit about real estate tax benefits can actually put money in your pocket.

First, you should know that there will be little tax benefit for private *lenders* in your business. Equity investors will fare far better under the tax code. Interest paid to private lenders — whether it's paid monthly or in full at closing — is generally taxed at the highest possible rates. But with *equity investors* (as opposed to *lenders)*, there are several ways both you *and* your private investors can benefit tax-wise.

What's the best way to use the tax code to your benefit? *Provide your private investors with the highest tax-advantaged returns possible.* Currently the lowest taxed investments are dividends and long-term capital gains. The tax rate on dividends is currently as low as 5%, and the long-term capital gain tax rate is 10-15%.

Depreciation is another great tax benefit for private investors. Depreciation is a tax rule that permits you to deduct the cost basis of buildings and improvements over time against the income derived from those properties, thus reducing your taxable income (and ultimately your taxes) — *even if the property has appreciated in value.*

Depreciation can be a little confusing, so let's look at an example:

Net Operating Income of Project: $100,000 (distributable to investors)
Depreciation: $10,000
Taxable Income From Project: $90,000

The depreciation from this project (which, for LLC and LPs passes through to the private investors) has shielded $10,000 in income from taxation. If a private investor's income falls within the 30% tax bracket, the depreciation deduction has saved the investor $3,000 in tax liability.

Knowing a little bit about how taxes work can help you bring in more private money. If an investor asks questions or expresses concern about the tax treatment of their investment, it helps tremendously if you can provide competent answers.

To illustrate, I once had a private investor who had invested $200,000 with me. He was happy as a clam with his returns… until tax time rolled around. One day, I got an angry call from him: *"You're killing me on my taxes!"* I knew he was mad — not 'give me my investment money back' mad — but definitely miffed. I kicked into gear and fast…

I worked up an investment proposal that demonstrated how various investments would be taxed. He happily chose the investment with the smallest tax liability, even though it offered him only a slightly better after-tax rate of return. He soon invested an additional $300,000 with me.

The moral of this story — some factors matter more to investors than others. But it's a fair bet that most investors will not want to pay a penny more in taxes than they absolutely have to. If you can help your private investors prevent

Uncle Sam from taking some of their money, it may mean a lot to them. It also means a lot to you, in terms of doing business with those investors in the future.

Tax Stuff You Need To Know

First, let me say that if you don't have a good CPA or qualified tax advisor, the time to get one was *yesterday*. It always astonishes me, the number of real estate investors who do not seek professional tax help. Several years ago, I met a CPA at a networking function whose pithy advice still rings in my ears: She said to one investor: "You're crazy if you've got your *DBA* and you don't have your *CPA*."

Hire a professional tax advisor at the beginning, as you're setting up your business. Don't wait until you have a tax problem to get professional advice. Developing a positive and efficient working relationship with a competent tax advisor will help keep your costs reasonable and more importantly, help you build a profitable business.

In addition to helping you save money and pay lower taxes, tax advisors can be worth their weight in gold simply by keeping you and your private investors on the right side of Uncle Sam. Nothing will throw cold water on your business faster than getting tangled up in an IRS audit or having some state government representative pay you an unfriendly visit.

Now that you've swallowed the hard medicine, let's look at some of the nitty gritty details…

Get Everything Set Up The Right Way

One of the first things you need to do when you get a private investor is to get their complete tax information. Have them complete a simple form that includes their name, address and social security number. If the investor questions this, just let them know — politely, of course — that you do everything by the book and you need this information to provide them with the documentation they'll need to for filing tax returns. You don't want your private investors to get a visit from the taxman, either.

Bookkeeping and Recordkeeping

For entrepreneurs, records and bookkeeping are about as popular as root canals. But keeping good records is the best way to steer clear of trouble down the road. What's the best record-keeping method to use? The one that your tax advisor prefers.

Here's a basic checklist to get you started:

- In order to ensure appropriate liability protection, you must maintain a separate checking account (do not co-mingle funds!) and maintain separate records for each of your real estate investments/projects
- Obtain an EIN and continue to maintain that legal entity
- If more than one party is involved and allocations are complex, you should engage legal counsel to draft the paperwork. A copy of this paperwork should also be provided to your tax advisor
- The most important document that you can provide your tax advisor for a new investment is a copy of the settlement statement you signed at closing
- Maintain careful records on any improvements made to acquisitions (such as describing the nature of the improvement). Your tax advisor must be able to determine, based on IRS parameters, the appropriate depreciation period and method to use

Providing your tax advisor with organized records will maximize his or her value to your business. Tax professionals are usually happy to teach you and/or refer you to a trained bookkeeper. Also, there are many inexpensive bookkeeping products on the market (Quickbooks® and MS Excel works) that can help you learn and keep you organized.

Annual Reporting & Filing Requirements

Each type of private investment in your business will come with its own tax reporting and filing requirements. Be sure to check with your CPA for specifics.

For Private Lenders

When you have private lenders, you're required to issue a form 1099 INT to them for any interest you paid them during the tax year. To issue a 1099 INT to your private investors, you'll need to file a form 1096 with the IRS. The 1096 informs the IRS how much interest income your private lender has received from you. In the instance of a private lender who has money loaned to different business entities, each business entity that has paid more than $600 per year in interest to the lender will have to issue a separate 1099 INT.

A funny quirk with the tax code is that even if your private lender accrues interest — meaning that they aren't paid any interest until the property sells — they are required to pay taxes on the interest earned. Here's an example of how this works…

If the private investor loaned $80,000 and was to be repaid $100,000 in three years, the IRS would consider the private investor to have earned $6,666.67 *per year* in interest income. Accordingly, a 1099 INT must be filed each year.

Remember, only the amount of *interest* paid to the lender is taxable to them as income and deductible as an expense by you. Any principal repayment is *not* taxed by the IRS and is *not* tax deductible. For instance, if you pay your lender $1,000 per month on an amortized loan, and the payments break down into $800 interest and $200 principal, only the $800 is deductible by you and taxable for the lender.

Private Equity Investors
If you have private equity investors, the most common tax form you will be issuing to them is a Schedule K-1. The K-1 details for the investor and the IRS the profits, losses and capital invested or withdrawn from the partnership. If your private investor is a member in your LLC, a limited partner in a partnership that you manage, you'll need to issue a Schedule K-1 to the investor.

Distributions from a C-corporation to shareholders are called *dividends*. If you have shareholders in a C-corporation, you must issue to them a 1099-DIV for any dividends issued during the tax year.

Keep It All Together
As you do private money deals, remember: using the tax laws to your advantage starts with good recordkeeping. Depending on the deal type and your private investor's tax status, the tax impact of various private money structures can help make a deal much more appealing. Structuring the deal for the private investor's best overall after-tax gain helps ensure that you have steady streams of private money coming your way.

Chapter 18

Securities Laws

I know what you're thinking — "Do I *really* have to trudge through securities legalese?" Technically, no. But if you don't, you just might end up in a ton of trouble. The goal, after all, is to get private money and start accumulating wealth, not spend every penny you make on attorney fees and regulatory filings (or worse).

Like it or not, we live in a nation of laws. Many of them are good (Imagine if we had no stop signs at intersections), but some of them leave us scratching our heads. There are laws to govern practically any activity you can think of — from traffic laws and consumer protections to, of course, real estate transactions. No one is immune. No business can operate successfully if it defies the regulations of its industry.

As an entrepreneur dealing with other people's money, your activities will be subject to several sections of U.S Securities code. You may be thinking that as long as you're not committing fraud or conducting business unethically, you don't need to be concerned about regulatory paperwork and securities mumbo jumbo. Wrong! You might be as honest as the day is long, but if you're not in compliance with securities laws, you're still operating illegally, which also means you're violating the Private Money Attraction Principles of *Integrity* and *Transparency*. You're setting yourself up for a fall.

Ignoring or complaining about the laws won't help you. If you want to change the laws, get yourself elected to political office. If you want to make money, learn how to comply with the laws in the most efficient, cost-effective way possible.

But please understand… even if you're just putting together your first private money deal or you are working on an initial public offering for your real estate investment trust (REIT), do *not* let the securities laws discourage you from pursuing private money. You can operate quite profitably within the government's legal framework.

This chapter will introduce you to basic securities laws, show you how they affect your efforts to raise private money and provide strategies that will help you remain in compliance with those laws. Since I'm not an attorney (thankfully), please note the disclaimer at the beginning of this book. Keep a good attorney on speed dial. When it comes to securities laws, you definitely don't want to mess around.

What the Heck is a 'Security,' Anyway?
A *security* is a negotiable financial instrument. Put more simply: a security is any form of investment from one person or company into another. Following are some examples of securities:

- Stocks
- Bonds
- Mutual Funds
- Promissory Notes
- Private Placements

When raising money for your real estate deals, promissory notes, and private placements are the securities you'll bump into most frequently. When you're dealing with other people's money, you're almost always dealing with securities. Therefore, it is commonly accepted that:

Any time you use private money, you are considered to be *selling a security*.

Why Do The Securities Laws Apply To Me?
Thanks to the good people at Ponzi Incorporated, Madoff Enterprises, and their subsidiary companies, we're all subject to securities laws. These fraudsters and their ilk create the need for such laws, creating more work for everybody — including those of us who conduct business with integrity.

Federal and state governments have deemed it in the public's best interest to enact laws and regulations to protect people from fraudulent investment schemes. As the Bernie Madoff fiasco illustrates, regulators don't always succeed, but the goal is to prevent all investors from getting burned.

Prior to 1933, there were no federal securities laws. Anybody and everybody could sell a stock, bond or any other investment (real or not), to any willing buyer. *Caveat emptor* (buyer beware) was the rule of the day. Landmark pieces of legislation such as the Securities Act of 1933, the Exchange Act of

1934, and various amendments changed the face of investments in America forever. Today, more than ever, they significantly impact businesses big and small

Each state also has its own securities laws regulations, commonly called *Blue Sky Laws*. Blue Sky laws are enforced by agencies and departments that vary from state to state. No two states are exactly alike. Some states are stricter than others when it comes to disclosure requirements and limitations on offerings. You must be careful to comply with both federal *and* state securities laws when raising capital.

What Do I Need To Do?

The level of legal compliance and paperwork required of you is determined by the category of the security you are selling:

- It's a security that must be *registered* (involves lots of paperwork)
- It's a security that's *exempt from registration* (involves less paperwork)

In other words, your security is either exempt from registration or you're required to register it.

Generally, any security you issue (a promissory note, a share of stock, an LLC interest) will need to be registered with the SEC, *unless an exemption exists*. For example, when a company "goes public" and sells stock in an IPO or when a large corporation sells newly issued bonds on the open market, they are required to file long and detailed paperwork with the SEC (and any applicable state agencies).

Registering a security with the SEC requires meeting stringent standards. You must provide facts about your offering and who is offering it for sale to the public. Information required for SEC registration includes: describing the business and its assets, the nature of the security to be sold, information about the company's managers and audited financial statements. All registration statements and prospectuses filed with the SEC become publicly available after they're filed. These statements are then accessible online via the SEC's publicly available database.

---------------------------$$$$ **Resource** $$$$---------------------------
Learn more about how securities law work and
how you can raise money quickly and easily.
Enroll in the 10 week free email course just visit
www.TheBookonPrivateMoney.com.
---------------------------$$$$$$---------------------------

How Do I Know If I Need To Register or Not?
I'm going to punt this one. Often, you'll need to seek advice from a securities lawyer on a case-by-case basis. There are many gray areas here, subject to interpretations of the law. The legal solution can vary widely. Your securities lawyer should be able to tell you whether your security must be registered or whether you can sell it under an exemption.

Selling a security under an exemption doesn't give you a free ride on the paperwork. You must still file some documents with either your state regulator and/or the SEC and provide disclosure documents to your private investors. Exemptions from registration simply mean less paperwork and less stringent oversight and inspection of your securities offering.

Generally, if you want to do any of the following, you will likely have to register your securities offering:

- Raise money from investors who reside in states other than your own
- Invest in real estate projects in states other than your own
- Raise very large amounts of money
- Use general solicitation/advertising

Exemptions: How to Legally Offer a Security without Registering
Fortunately, most real estate investors can offer securities without going through the onerous torture of a full-blown SEC registration. There are many ways to legally offer a security without registering it with the SEC. If your offering qualifies for an *exemption* from registration requirements, you may not have to register (which means far less paperwork and lower cost). Following is a summary of some of the most frequently used securities law exemptions:

Regulation D
Regulation D or "Reg D," as it's known in securities law slang, is probably the most frequently used exemption by real estate investors. There are three primary sections of Reg D that you should be aware of:

> *Section 504* – Is an exemption for the offer and sale of up to $1,000,000 of securities in a 12-month period. With Rule 504, you may not advertise to the public to sell your securities. Under most circumstances, any investors who purchase securities from you under Rule 504 cannot sell them without exemption or registration.

Section 505 - This rule provides an exemption for offering and selling securities for amounts up to $5 million in any 12-month period. You cannot use advertisements or general solicitations to sell securities when you use this exemption. Under Rule 505, you can sell your securities to an unlimited number of 'accredited investors' and up to 35 non-accredited investors.

Section 506 - Rule 506 allows you to raise unlimited amounts of capital, sell securities to accredited investors and non-accredited investors (up to 35). The information, sale restriction, and information disclosure requirements, including financial statements are similar to Rule 505. The main difference between Rule 506 and Rule 505 is that any non-accredited investor you sell securities to must meet sophistication requirements (more on this in a minute).

Regulation A

Regulation A is an exemption for *public* securities offerings not exceeding $5 million in any 12-month period. Regulation A exemptions have some stringent requirements, but with those requirements come some advantages over full registration, such as:

- No reporting obligations to comply with the Exchange Act after the offering (unless your company has more than $10 million in total assets and more than 500 shareholders)
- Audited financial statements are not required
- Simplified offering circular format — you can use a question and answer format
- "Testing the waters" is allowed

"Testing the waters" means that the SEC allows you to advertise your offering to the general public before you file your documents with them. However, there's a Catch-22: You can't take any money from investors until you have filed your forms with the SEC, the SEC has reviewed them, and you have provided the documents to the investors. The upside is that testing the waters allows you to gauge interest for your offering before going through the entire paperwork process or paying any filing fees to the SEC.

Intrastate Offering Exemption

When operating under an intrastate exemption, there are no limits on the amount of money you can raise or the number of purchasers you can have. Under this exemption, you must not sell to anyone outside your state. Note that it's your responsibility to verify that whomever you sell securities to is, in fact, a resident of *your* state.

Who is Accredited? Who is Sophisticated?

When researching securities laws, you'll often see the terms "accredited investor" and "sophisticated investor." Following are general descriptions of each of these two categories of private investor:

Accredited Investor[xiv]

- a bank, insurance company, registered investment company, business development company, or small business investment company;
- an employee benefit plan — within the meaning of the Employee Retirement Income Security Act, if a bank, insurance company, or registered investment adviser makes the investment decisions, or if the plan has total assets in excess of $5 million;
- a charitable organization, corporation or partnership with assets exceeding $5 million;
- a director, executive officer, or general partner of the company selling the securities;
- a business in which all the equity owners are accredited investors;
- a natural person with a net worth of at least $1 million;
- a natural person with income exceeding $200,000 in each of the two most recent years or joint income with a spouse exceeding $300,000 for those years and a reasonable expectation of the same income level in the current year; or
- a trust with assets of at least $5 million, not formed to acquire the securities offered, and whose purchases are directed by a sophisticated person.

Sophisticated Investor

Sophisticated investors are: "*those who have enough knowledge and experience in finance and business matters to evaluate the risks and merits of the investment.*"[xv] Pretty simple, right?

Who In Their Right Mind Would *Want* to Register Their Security?

Now, you may be asking — *Why wouldn't everyone just operate under an exemption, instead of enduring the annoyance of registration?* First of all, companies that want to raise big money or use general solicitations to find investors will probably need to register their securities. Even though the registration process takes time and effort, registration is appealing on several levels; for instance:

- You can raise an unlimited amount of money
- You can advertise your offering
- You may be able to sell your securities through broker/dealers

When you start raising larger amounts of amounts of money, the exemption provisions start to become unfeasible. It's easier to go ahead and execute the registration process. Also, many real estate investors want to capitalize on various advertising media (internet, radio, etc.) to attract investors. Promotional solicitations can be a profitable lead generator, if you properly market your opportunity.

Another reason to register your security is that some broker/dealers may be able to sell your security to their clients. A securities broker/dealer is a company that trades securities for its own account, or on behalf of its clients. Essentially, a securities broker/dealer employs licensed securities salespeople who generate income by selling securities. Typically, securities salespeople earn commissions on the securities they sell. Since broker/dealers are heavily regulated, most will not offer your security for sale to their clients unless it's registered with the SEC.

A broker/dealer may offer your securities in exchange for a commission on sale. When your security is registered, you can legally pay commissions to licensed brokers for selling your security. Usually, if you're operating under an exemption you can't pay commissions or referral fees to those who bring investors to you.

A broker dealer can potentially unleash a flood of investors and remove the burden of marketing and selling your securities from you. Many broker dealers have clients who are ready, willing, and able to invest money into your real estate business. This could be a good avenue for you to explore at some point, especially when you want to raise a lot of money.

A Few Additional Points…

Advertising

We've touched on advertising compliance before, but it bears repeating: if you advertise to the general public (people you don't know) for private money, you must make sure your advertising complies with the securities laws. Work with a good securities lawyer to make sure your advertising language is legal.

If you run newspaper ads claiming that investors can earn 10% on their money with your real estate investment, an official from your state securities regulator (or perhaps a federal regulator) may take notice of your ad — now you're on their radar screen! And you don't want that. You could potentially be subject to cease and desist orders and/or a detailed examination of your business operation.

That said, don't let anybody tell you that you're not allowed to advertise for private money — you most certainly *can* advertise for private money. *As long as you're compliant with any applicable securities laws.* This may mean you'll need to file offering statements with state and federal regulators and submit filing fees and other requirements (such as audited financial statements).

Can't I just use my regular attorney?

If your attorney handles evictions and real estate closings, can he or she handle the securities compliance aspects of your business as well? Maybe. However, chances are, if your attorney isn't a specialist in securities law, they may not have the necessary expertise. It's kind of like asking a general family internist to perform an angioplasty. But, do you really want him to? Or would you prefer that a cardiologist or cardiothoracic surgeon perform your angioplasty? Unless you're having a sudden coronary at Disneyland and the internist is the only one who raises his hand when someone yells, "Is anyone a doctor?" you'd probably prefer the cardiac specialist.

When you get serious about taking and using other people's money in your business, you need to work with an attorney who specializes in securities law. Scrutinize his or her education, experience and client list. Note the types of transactions they've handled.

Is a Securities Attorney Going to Cost Me My Firstborn?

Here's the answer to your next question: No, securities lawyers don't come cheap. Well, some might, but when it comes to attorneys, it's been my experience that you get what you pay for. Instead of shopping price-only, shop reputation and specialized securities expertise. Good securities lawyers know what they're doing and will be quick and efficient in getting you what you need — as long as you understand what that is, which brings me to my next point…

Protection, Not a Deterrent

Don't view securities laws as a deterrent to raising private money. Legal compliance is just part of the cost of doing business. If you owned a manufacturing company, you'd have to comply with OSHA and environmental laws. Make it a point to be generally aware of what's required of you. And retain a good attorney to help you deal with more complex matters. Look at it this way: Securities laws protect the public from fraudsters who bilk money from investors who could have invested that money in *your* business. The securities laws that we all grumble about may, in fact, be protecting our private investors and family members from the next Ponzi.

Final Thoughts

Y ou either get it or you don't...

By now, you either understand, embrace and are excited about the power that private money can bring to your real estate investing business, or you don't. There really isn't a middle ground. In fact, middle ground is never a good place to be in business.

Whenever I talk to real estate investors about private money, I can see my message click for some and bounce right off others. Some entrepreneurs immediately connect the dots and others simply do not.

I find this is analogous to the movie *The Matrix*. *The Matrix* is about a group of people who fight to take down a computer-generated world that holds virtually all of humanity hostage from birth in order to harness energy. The hero of *The Matrix* is a character named "Neo." Neo is thought to be the missing link needed by the humans to finally defeat the computers.

Neo doesn't believe that he is really "The One", but, near the end of the movie, he finally sees the computer-generated world for what it is: an amalgamation of 1s and 0's. Once he *sees* what the Matrix really is, 1's and 0's, he is unstoppable against anything the computers can throw at him.

Once you see the power of private money, you see the 1's and 0's of real estate investing and, just like *The Matrix*, there is nothing that can stop you. There are deals I have done that I never would have even heard about —all because of private money. It's truly the "Holy Grail' of real estate investing. But, the best part is, you don't have to go looking under thousands of years of ancient gravel and rock for it, you can plug into the principles, methods, and techniques described in this book and have private money in your business in short order.

We've covered a lot of ground throughout this book. However, even if I dedicated ten books to the subject of private money, it simply wouldn't be enough to cover every possible detail. There is a great deal of learning beyond this book that you will have to do on your own. There are only two directions in business: forward and backward. There is no neutral.

However, there is a caveat that must come with all types of learning: you have to *implement* what you learn or it won't matter. Learning is great. Learning is fun. But learning is just potential energy waiting to be released. You must *take action* on what you learn. Otherwise, it just sits in your head and then evaporates into your gray matter.

The business sidelines are full of what I call 'wantrapreneurs' –wanna-be entrepreneurs. These are people that have every intention of starting a business, buying a piece of investment real estate, but they just can't get out of the starting blocks. They've gone to all the classes, taken all the home study courses, but they still don't have any money in their pocket to show for it.

In order to cross over from 'wantrapreneur' to entrepreneur, you have to *take action*. It can be scary, un-nerving or frustrating at times, but there is just no substitute for the feeling you get after you close a profitable deal. Walking away from the closing table with a huge check or closing on a multi-million dollar purchase is something very few people will ever experience. The reason so few people experience this is simple: action.

Think back about this: what if I offered to give you a penny? "Big deal," you'd probably think. But, what if I offered to start you with a penny and double your amount each day for one month? For instance, on day one, you'd have $.01; day two = $0.02, day four = $0.08, and so on. How much money would you have at the end of the month?

You'd have over *$5.3 million!* That's right: doubling the penny every day doesn't add up to much at first (on day 15 it's only worth $163 bucks). However, the daily compounding effect leads to a substantial sum after just 30 days. This example is one of my favorites for showing how much power *our daily actions* have over the results we want.

If you commit yourself to taking at least one positive action toward acquiring private money each day, no mater how small you think it might be; for example, putting up your website or going to a networking function, you will be amazed at the results you will get. The daily actions you take can compound *for you* and the daily actions you don't take can compound *against you*.

The best thing is that *you can make the choice*. You can choose to use private money to take your business to the next level or not. You can choose financial independence or not. You can choose to take action or let the knowledge sit idle and then fade away.

It's up to you.

Bonus Chapter #1

Using the Other Half of Your Investing Brain

Just about every real estate investor uses only *half their brain* when it comes to private money and it costs them dearly...

In Chapter 1 we discussed two sides of the private money coin: private money *loans* and private money *equity* investments. Although the analogy was two sides of the same coin, even more so than that we're really talking about *two sides of your brain*.

Just about every real estate investor under the sun, moon and stars thinks of private money only in terms of private *loans* and they never think of *equity* investors. Considering the profits involved, this is quite puzzling. Essentially, if you're only thinking in terms of private money *loans* you are only using HALF YOUR BRAIN.

A massive profit breakthrough in my real estate business really came when I started thinking with both sides of my brain. In fact, I no longer even take in private money in the form of loans or mortgages. Every single dollar of private money I take is in the form of an equity investment. Each new private investor that comes into my business now is making a great investment by receiving an interest in an LLC, a preferred stock investment in a C-corporation, or purchasing units in a limited partnership.

I didn't always think this way. When I first started getting private money, I beat my drum to the same beat you are probably familiar with: a promissory note secured by a mortgage or trust deed. However, I started to get really hamstrung by this approach. Actually, it was worse than that: having only private money *lenders* was actually *costing me money!*

Show Me the Money

Each time I used private loans to close a deal, I would have to go to my private lenders, have them fund the loan, set up all the loan paperwork, do the closing at the title company, pay to have the mortgage recorded and so on. This might seem like no big deal, but when you're buying and selling 6-8 houses per month, and turning over the private money for those deals at least once a month in the process, you can see how burdensome it can become. The costs of keeping up with all of this meant I had to spend more time (remember time = money) and also pay my office assistant for more hours. All of this meant less take home money for me each month.

Another problem was I had to give the private loan money back to the private investor after each deal closing. I would borrow money to purchase the property. Then, when the property sold 30-45 days later, I would have to repay the private money loan and have a check cut back to the private investor at closing. The issue with this was the investors wanted to keep their money invested and continually earning interest. With the money turnover I was generating in my business, it was a real pain to keep giving money back and then get it invested again.

The real kicker was that having things set up with my investors in the form of private money loans was costing me the ability to do more deals. Each time I made an offer on a bank owned property, I needed to provide them a "Proof of Funds." Since I was making "all cash" offers (not contingent on any form of financing), I needed to show the seller I had the ability to pay cash to close quickly on the property. By not having the proof of funds that the REO (foreclosure) banks and asset managers wanted, I was losing out on deals that would have put thousands of dollars in my pocket.

It wasn't too long ago that banks used to accept a letter written from a private investor that told them that they had committed funds for a deal. As the inventory of bank owned homes began to swell, banks and asset managers began to only accept a verifiable company bank statement (from the company making the offer) with the requisite funds in the account to close the deal. For the most part, these sellers only wanted to deal with cash buyers. Letters from the private investor stating they had committed the necessary funds for the deal no longer cut it.

As you might be able to guess, this was problematic because it essentially meant I had to have the funds to close any given deal in my business bank account to make an all cash offer that would get taken seriously. Since I didn't have $600,000+ in my business operating account at the time, I was in a bind to get my offers in the hands of the real decision makers. It wasn't enough to have a bank or account statement from one of my private investors' accounts (which was a big pain in the rear, anyway). There was no escaping the fact that I had to have the cash in my company account necessary to close every deal I was offering "all cash" on.

---————————$$$$ Resource $$$$————————---
Find out how to structure your deals for maximum profit
and maximum private money (it's a lot easier than you think).
www.TheBookonPrivateMoney.com.
———————————$$$$$$———————————

Cash is King

The best deals were (and still very much are) when you pay 'all cash'. There are no two ways about it: money talks. When I turned my sites on bigger investment deals, like apartment buildings, it was very clear that having the funds on hand when making a cash offer was the only way it was going to get put through. Even for the apartment deals where I was going to use commercial loan financing for part of the acquisition, the initial equity and working capital requirements had to be on hand for my bank to take my loan application package seriously.

I'm the first one to acknowledge the infinite ways in which you can acquire real estate make it one of the best businesses to be in. There are literally dozens and dozens of techniques to acquire properties, from single-family houses to office buildings, using creative financing techniques that don't require any up-front cash. I have employed many of these techniques myself to varying degrees during my investing career.

Without equivocation, I have to say that the "all cash" approach to acquiring single-family houses and having the dry powder on hand to easily obtain commercial financing for a big project have been *far and away* the most profitable investing technique I have used. I have made a great deal more money by raising private money and then acquiring properties than any other purchasing method out there. There is a reason why they say: "cash is king."

Why Would a Private Investor Do This?

Why would a private investor trade a secured loan on a property for an equity ownership? After all, this probably flies in the face of everything you thought about private money before you picked up this book. Here are a few reasons:

Equity Investment is Easier for the Private Investor

They don't have to worry about notes, mortgages and other paperwork. The investment is as simple as if they owned a mutual fund or shares of stock in a public company. They continue to get monthly statements and are paid their returns almost the same as a loan.

The Investor Becomes Your Partner

For a lot of private investors, the prospect of 'partnering' on deals is more appealing than being a lender. I simply told my investors that they would in fact be the partial owners of each property my company purchased. I told them they could drive by each property and tell their friends or anyone else that it was a property *they* owned. Giving investors a sense of 'pride of ownership' and making them partners in your business is very attractive.

Billionaire investor Warren Buffett uses the 'partner' concept to a great extent with his company, Berkshire Hathaway. Buffett even refers to Berkshire Hathaway shareholders as "partners"[xvi] and goes to great lengths to make this a part of the culture of his multi-hundred-billion dollar global empire. It works like a charm, too. Many investors have owned their Berkshire Hathaway stock for decades and refuse to sell even when the price of their shares takes a beating in the stock market.

Investors Like the Idea of Being a Part of Something Big

It's no secret that people like the thought of a big upside. When you have an equity investor in your business that shares in the profits and cash flow, they have a chance to make a larger return than if they just made a fixed interest rate loan.

Collateral is Not As Important As You Might Think

The simple fact is very few private investors have any interest in foreclosing on a property if you go bad on a loan. Even though the security of a mortgage makes for nice window dressing when proposing an investment, in practical terms it's not going to mean much to most private investors. It's got a lot of 'bark' and very little 'bite'.

Foreclosing on a house they loaned money on so they can sell it to recoup their investment is not very appealing to most people. After all, what really happens when a private investor has to foreclose? They first have to hire an attorney and then begin the legal process to take back the property. Depending on the state you are doing business in and records the private investor has kept, the process for the investor to get the house back could take up to six months or longer.

After the investor legally gains ownership to the house, they then have the job of making that house ready for sale. Provided that the house is in reasonable condition and the market is active, the private investor would have to hire a real estate agent to list and sell the house. Considering all the costs, time and hassle of doing this, how much do you think your private lender is going to like the thought of foreclosing if the deal goes bad? They may not even recoup their entire investment principal.

On the other hand, banks and other lending institutions are in the business of loaning money. As such, they have the resources and financial means to foreclose and sell properties to try to recoup their loan principal. Private lenders don't have these same capabilities. Basically, a private investor is investing in the strength of *you*, *your business*, *your deals,* and *your ability to make money for them.*

Private Investors Like Paying Less in Taxes
As we touched on earlier, there are definite tax advantages for private investors who have equity interests versus loans. Interest paid or accrued to a private lender over $600 per year is taxable to them as ordinary income. Let's say you paid a distribution to a limited partner of $10,000 per year. Due to depreciation alone, perhaps only $8,000 or less of the $10,000 partnership distribution will be taxable. Also, the profits on any properties held for at least 12 months and sold for a gain are treated as long-term capital gains, which (currently) have much lower tax rates than ordinary income.

The Evolution of the Revolution
I began transitioning my business to equity capital funding by converting my existing private lenders into equity investors. Each time one of them had their promissory notes paid off at the closing of a deal, I would retain the cash and, in exchange, they received shares of stock in a C-corporation I had previously set up. For their stock investment, they received a quarterly dividend payment and a percentage ownership interest in the company.

Even though I faced some issues with 'double taxation' because I used a C-corporation, the net tax impact was very minimal. Because we were flipping so many houses held for under 12 months (taxed as ordinary income), our total income taxes paid came out about the same as it would if we had used a limited liability company or a limited partnership. We were also able to utilize other tax benefits C-corps enjoy that limited liability companies (LLCs) and limited partnerships (LPs) do not, which helped reduce the overall tax burden.

The dividend payments my private investors received along with the ownership interest in the corporation provided many of them with even better returns on their money than they were receiving as lenders. On top of that, they got to keep more of their money as well, since the dividend payments they received were taxed at a lower rate than the interest payments they were previously getting.

The first step that I took to make all this happen was to put together a proposal for my existing lenders. I laid out for them the benefits of being an equity investor in my business: higher returns on investment, tax benefits, less paperwork. I sat down with each of them and went through the entire proposal. Most of them liked it and were eager to get started.

Next, I got some input from my securities lawyer about how to handle the paperwork for the equity investment, had the documents drafted and then presented them formally to my soon-to-be equity investors. Once they signed off on the offering documents, it was simply a matter of moving the money from one entity to the next via certified checks handled by a title company.

A Maverick Approach
When I first talked about converting my lenders into equity investors, some people thought I was nuts. They thought it was a little too 'unconventional.' When I talked to other seasoned real estate investors I knew in my local area, they had absolutely no clue what I was talking about. I took great solace in this. It's a good general rule that if everybody is doing one thing or everybody thinks one thing is the best, it's better to go the *other* direction.

So, my approach to raising private money for real estate deals (and my entire business model for that matter) became: "ready, fire, aim." I focused on getting the money *first* and then getting the deals. My profits went up immensely after I adopted this approach.

Keep It Simple
It's just as easy to get a private equity investor in your business (sometimes easier) as it is to get a secured private lender. There may be other people that want you to believe otherwise, but I'm living proof this just isn't the case. Remember, you can raise the money and go after deals at the same time. The biggest and best investors in the world use this approach.

If you think this is out of reach for you because you are just getting started investing, think again! This strategy is more applicable to you than anybody else because you can get started on the right foot. What a relief to get out of the gate the right way and not have to correct when you're out there in the trenches doing deals. The time to get it right is when you're in the *starting* blocks.

Don't get me wrong - private money loans are just fine. You should *never* turn away private money, because you're going to close way more deals and make a lot of profits with it. For me, equity investors are preferable in almost every way to private lenders.

If Equity Investors Are So Great, Why Doesn't Everyone Do It?
Why don't more real estate investors use equity capital for private money? I have identified three primary reasons:

1. They are conditioned to think only in terms of loans
2. They don't want to give up a piece of the action (otherwise known as being 'penny wise and pound foolish')
3. They don't know how to properly set up the deal

Thinking only in terms of loans
When you first learn about investing, you learn that going to a bank and getting a loan is the basic way of acquiring real estate. After you learn about real estate investing more, you hear things about private money lending or private mortgage lending. There is very little talk or discussion about raising private equity capital for real estate deals. This is unfortunate – but we can remedy that, can't we?

Not Wanting to Give up a Piece of the Action
I don't know about you, but I'd rather have a smaller piece of something big than a big piece of something small. Most real estate entrepreneurs could reason this as well. Some don't want to give up part of the profits or cash flows on a deal no matter what. This is despite the fact that they are giving up profits and cash flows anyway if they are paying interest on a loan (whether to a bank or private lender).

When you bring an equity investor in, you are sharing with them the profits and cash flows of the project(s) you invest in with their money. The percentage of the project or deal you give to the investor depends on many factors: the type of deal, amount of money needed, time frame and risk level. The thought of not giving up a part of the deal to get the capital is small minded and short-sighted. This is what is called being 'penny wise and pound foolish.'

Not Knowing How to Set Up the Deal
There are big differences in setting up deals with a loan versus equity investment. For instance, how much of the deal or how much of your company should the private investor get in exchange for their investment? What sort of returns should be paid?

The easiest way I found to set up deals with equity investors was to determine the amount of money I wanted to make and then work the private investors return into the equation. If the deal made sense for me and my private investors, I move on it. If the numbers didn't work, I give it a pass. Here's an example:

Let's say you're looking at acquiring a 40-unit apartment building

Figure 19.1

Private Equity - 40 Unit Apartment Purchase	
Purchase Price	$1,000,000
Annual Net Cash Flow	$150,000
Commercial Financing (65% purchase price)	$650,000
Equity Requirement at Closing	$350,000
Operating Capital Needed	$150,000
Private Money Needed	**$500,000**

As Figure 19.1 shows, you're purchasing the property for $1,000,000. You have a commercial mortgage for $650,000, so you need $350,000 for the down payment at closing. In addition, you need $150,000 in operating capital, for some repairs, closing costs, and a reserve account.

You've decided (in exchange for your upfront and ongoing time involvement) that you want to make $25,000 per year from this project. Subtracting this $25,000 from the $150,000 annual cash flow leaves $125,000 to distribute to your private investors. If the private investors brought the $500,000 and received $125,000 per year, they would be earning about 25% per year on their money.

Essentially, you're carving about 17% of the deal for yourself and distributing the remainder to your investors. If you brought 10 private investors that each invested $50,000, you'd distribute $125,000 amongst them each year ($12,500 per investor). I personally don't know many private investors that would sneeze at a 25% annual return on investment! By analyzing the numbers with your and your private investors interests in mind, you can quickly see which deals make sense and which ones do not.

You could set this deal up in many ways from a legal entity standpoint. You could use a limited partnership (with your company as the general partner) or you could set it up as a limited liability company with you as the manager and your investors as members. These are just a few of the structures I have used for deals like this. Be sure to consult a qualified attorney before you set everything up. It stings your wallet if you have to re-do things and it also delays the deal.

As you can see, a deal like the example we just went through works all the way around. It's a true 'win-win'; your private investors make a good return on their investment and you turn a nice profit. If you really want to put your business in overdrive, put the money together up-front and then pursue the deal. You have more negotiating power this way and you're in a better position with the seller of the building and your commercial financing source.

Use Both Sides of Your Brain

When you're ready to take your business to the next level or get a head start out of the gate, use equity investors. The benefits of using equity investors as opposed to private lenders are many. You can position yourself to take advantage of deals you never could have before and provide your investors with tax-advantaged returns on their money.

Perhaps the most convincing argument is that the biggest real estate investment companies, publicly traded REITS (real estate investment trusts) and other big players all heavily utilize equity investors. If you want to have a big and profitable company, it helps to model yourself after big and profitable companies.

Tap into the power of my "Ready, Fire, Aim" approach to acquiring real estate. If you put the money together and then pursue the deals, you'll land a much higher percentage of the choicest projects. After all, who wants to go hunting with no gun and no ammunition?

Bonus Chapter #2

The Goose That Laid the Golden Eggs

It's a well known but sad fact that many small businesses (real estate investors included) do not have a business plan. According to the U.S. Small Business Administration, only 50% of businesses survive their first five years. One of the most often cited reasons for this is lack of adequate business planning.[xvii]

I will admit that I used to be firmly in the 'I don't need a business plan' camp. Everything I needed to succeed buying and selling real estate was on the back of a Starbucks® napkin. I thought fancy business plans were only for companies that were trying to get big venture capital financing or for Silicon Valley start-ups. How on earth could you even make a business plan for a real estate investing company?

It didn't take long for the importance of a business plan to hit me over the head like a ton of bricks. All it took was for a potential whale of a private investor to ask me about one and I was scrambling around looking under every rock and searching every website and getting every book that would help me get a good business plan for this investor.

Eventually, I developed a business plan that worked for both private money as well as bank financing for real estate. It wasn't without getting some firm rebukes in the process, though. Over time, I began advising other real estate investors and business owners, helping them develop winning business plans.

My personal experience and the experience and success of my consulting clients with business planning was profound. I found that the better my business plan was, the more successful my business became. It helped me get the financing I needed, organize my business better, control costs, and get an overall sense of confidence about the direction I was steering my company.

All told, my business plan has resulted in millions of dollars in business for my company. This is why I call it "The Goose That Laid the Golden Eggs." I want to share with you some of the key aspects of a winning business plan for a real estate investing business. Before you jump too far ahead of me, please know this: it doesn't matter what type of deals you want to do or how big of a business you want to have – a business plan will help you greatly, in more ways than you will realize at the outset.

Getting Started

Getting started with a business plan is simply a matter of putting your thoughts down on paper. You are simply putting together a skeleton and gradually adding to it. Don't put too much pressure on yourself. Just grab a blank tablet of legal paper (or your laptop), a pen, and sit in a quiet spot.

Here are a few things to think about:

- What type of deals are you going to do? (flip, single family rental, multi-family, etc.)
- How will you find your deals?
- How will you sell or rent your houses?
- How will you finance your deals?
- How many deals have you done so far?
- What professionals have you hired? (accountants, attorney, etc.)
- What is your goal for profits in 1, 3 and 5 years?
- Why did you start investing in real estate?
- What real estate or other business experience do you have?

Writing down your answers to the questions above will get you started thinking about what you must include in your business plan.

Business Plan Structure

There are many ways you can structure your business plan. While there are no concrete structures that you absolutely *must use*, there are some basic components that I think should be included in every solid business plan. They are as follows:

- Executive Summary
- Marketing Plan
- Financial Plan
- Operating Plan

Executive Summary

The executive summary is the first part of your business plan that will be read. It summarizes your entire business and gives key highlights and milestones. The main purpose of the executive summary is to clearly and concisely capture the opportunity you are pursuing, how you will make money from that opportunity and what will be required to achieve the profits you believe are possible from pursuing it.

In your business, the opportunity may be bank-owned single family homes, government subsidized multi-family apartment buildings or land development. If we use bank owned single-family homes as an example, the executive summary should communicate how you plan on profiting from investing in them, and what resources it will take to do it. You would include the approximate inventory of bank owned homes in your market, how you plan to buy them and how much profit there is to be made by either flipping them or renting them.

Your executive summary should entice the reader to read through your plan in its entirety. In fact, it may be best to think of your executive summary as the 'teaser' for your business plan – an interesting synopsis that will pull the reader in the fold and get them involved in learning more about your business.

Even though your executive summary is the first part of your business plan that will be read, it is the *last* part that you will complete. It is much easier to write an executive summary after you have completed the other components of your plan – since you will essentially just be summarizing those separate parts.

Marketing Plan

The marketing plan is probably the most comprehensive aspect of your business plan. Most entrepreneurs make the mistake of thinking the marketing plan is simply a summary of the advertising they will run or the promotions they will use. While advertising and promotions are critical, they are only one piece of the marketing plan. Your marketing plan should concisely describe the market for the real estate deals you will pursue, the characteristics of that market, quantify the market, and then show how you will attract and retain business within the market.

For example, if your business is acquiring multi-family apartment buildings, your marketing plan would include things like: your target geography, the number of multi-family units in the area, the absorption rate, the average rents and vacancies, along with how you will find the deals and then attract tenants to the buildings you will buy.

The advertising and promotions part of your marketing plan should include how you will market and sell your houses or fill vacancies. It should also have details about how you will find your properties and ensure you are getting good deals. The marketing plan usually requires you to do a little bit of homework. Knowing your market well is important to operating profitably and gaining the confidence of private investors.

Financial Plan

The financial plan is the most fun part of your business plan. This is the section where you show how the deals you will do result in profits year after year. You can include detailed profit projections as well as summarize the sources and uses of capital that you require. Be sure to include the assumptions you are making in generating your projected results.

For instance, if you are flipping single-family houses, show how many houses you will need to flip in order to achieve your profit goal. Also, remember to include details about how much money you will need from private investors and how these amounts tie back to the number of deals you will do.

Don't go too overboard on spreadsheets or complex financial projections. It can be easy to get carried away and have a lot of moving parts in this part of your plan. No matter how much detail you try to cover, you're still dealing with 'projections', which by their very nature are going to be a ballpark guide. The purpose of your financial plan is to flush out how much money you will need to hit your profit targets. Making it any more complicated than this is just inviting more headaches and time commitment than you need.

Operations Plan

The operations plan is the 'meat and potatoes' of your business plan. This section is where you will spell out exactly what you will do on a daily, weekly and monthly basis to make money. Be sure to describe what the responsibilities of various aspects of your business are and who will handle these responsibilities.

This section of your plan might take you the longest to complete. It is important that you think through the various operational details of your business so you have a plan that makes sense. Look for areas to delegate and identify problem areas where your operations could break down and solve these problems.

If your business was developing land, your operations plan might include the process for gaining various municipal and county approvals and permits, the process for subdividing the land and the process for bringing in roads, water/sewer, and other easements.

Other Business Plan Components

While the four previously discussed components are mandatory to include in your business plan, there are other parts you may want to include in your plan:

- Company description
- Personnel plan
- Management

The most important thing to remember is that you want your business plan to clearly capture the opportunity you are pursuing and how you will capitalize on it. Keep it simple and easy to understand.

$$$$ **Resource** $$$$
Get more business plan tips and techniques.
Go to *www.TheBookonPrivateMoney.com*
$$$$$$

Business Plan Taboos
Avoid doing the following in your business plan...

Rosy profit projections

One way to lose credibility quickly with an investor reading your business plan is to overstate the amount of money you anticipate making within the time period you set forth. For instance, making a million dollars per month in net income in the second year of business, while quite possible, may not fit in the context of your plan when you are starting out with your first deal.

There is nothing wrong with setting high goals for yourself. However, when you are looking for outside investors, you want to ensure that you don't lose their belief in you. Be somewhat conservative in your profit projections – it is always better to under-promise and over-deliver than the other way around.

Overusing Industry Lingo

A good rule of thumb is to write your plan so that even someone who has never heard of your business or industry could understand it. Avoid using terms, phrases, and jargon a layperson could not understand. If you do use industry specific terms, explain them.

Too many words

Utilize graphs, charts, tables, bullet points and pictures when possible to substitute for a wordy description. Many people understand things better when they have visual aids. People also can better digest large amounts of information if your plan is broken down into bits and pieces.

Missing pieces

Make sure you print and read your business plan through a few times before you give it to anyone to read, especially private investors. I advise having an independent person (a friend or family member) read your plan and provide some critiques for you. You would be surprised at what other people will find when they review your plan. They may help you plug holes, fix grammar and spelling, or ensure you explain some points in greater detail where needed.

Although on the surface it may seem li[xviii]ke a good idea to have your attorney or CPA review your plan, I recommend always having a non-professional proofread your plan. While your professional advisors will undoubtedly welcome the billable hours and provide you with sound guidance, you should have someone who fits the profile of your prospective private investor read through your plan and give you some objective feedback.

What if I don't want to write a business plan?

If the prospect of writing a business plan sounds daunting to you, don't worry. You do have some options if you understand the importance, but don't necessarily want to write your own business plan.

Consultants

You can hire a consultant, attorney or accountant to write one for you. Although this may be expensive, you can utilize their expertise and possibly circumvent some of the challenges you may encounter if you were to write it yourself. If you go this route, make sure you find out if the person you hire has a very sound knowledge of real estate investing – particularly the strategies you will use.

Although there are plenty of consultants and advisors out there, I have found that many professionals have no experience or understanding of the complicated and creative real estate investing strategies used, nor do they know how to properly communicate the opportunity to a private investor.

Software

Business planning software may also be an option. In my experience, business planning software can be a valuable formatting tool and can be helpful for steering you in the right direction when it comes to structuring your plan. There are some severe drawbacks to using software for writing your business plan.

For example, there are very few business plan software templates that fit well for real estate investing and most programs have certain rules that don't allow for much deviation from a pre-set structure. Another issue arises with regard to the financial plan component — I have yet to see a business planning software program that encompasses the right type of financial plan template for a real estate investing company.

If You Fail to Plan, You Can Plan to Fail

Having a business plan is very important to building the foundation and credibility you need to attract private money. In addition, having a business plan will provide you with a strong internal operating guideline that will help you handle issues that arise and better prepare you for any obstacles. Having a business plan that is clear, concise and accurate will put you in the minority of real estate investors – which means you are that much closer to getting all the private money you can handle.

How to Get More Information from the Author

FREE RESOURCES FOR THIS BOOK

To help you get more value from *The Book on Private Money*, there are many **FREE RESOURCES** for you to use – just visit…

www.TheBookonPrivateMoney.com

Resources you're entitled to are:

- **FREE Email Course…***10 weeks of free education*
- **FREE TELESEMINAR….***access to Members Only calls*
- **FREE WEBINAR -***Online Learning for maximum success*
- **FREE AUDIO CD '*SECRETS OF PRIVATE MONEY REVEALED'***

….all of this and MORE is ready for you at
www.TheBookonPrivateMoney.com

Special Free Gift for Taking Action

Complete and Fax this page to: 586-816-0470 or go to
www.TheBookonPrivateMoney.com

FREE *Private Money Mastery* Membership Enrollment

You get:
1. Two Free Issues of *Moneywire* Newsletter
2. Two Free Months Teleseminar Attendance
3. Ultimate Private Money Resources Access
4. Free Audio CD *Secrets of Private Money Revealed*
5. 10 Week Private Money email course

First Name:_____ Last Name:_____

Mailing Address: _____

City: _____ State:_____ Zip:_____

Email: _____ Phone: _____

Credit Card(check one): Visa____ Mastercard____ Amex____ Discover___

Card #_____

Exp. Date _____ CSV_____

Signature_____ Date _____

There will be a one-time charge of $4.95 for postage for two free months of the Private Money Mastery Program and you have no obligation to continue the monthly membership ($49.95 per month). You may continue your monthly membership and cancel at any time. Providing the information above grants your permission to Champions of Success, LLC to contact you regarding related information via the means listed above.

FREE ADMISSION!

EXCLUSIVE Private Money Conference

One-Day Private Money Education Event Where You'll Learn

- Where to find private investors
- How to structure deals
- How to raise over $5 million in 3 months or less
- More…

$997 Public Registration Fee

This coupon is valid for *2 Free Tickets*

Register at: *www.TheBookonPrivateMoney.com.* Click on "seminars." Use the following code:

DNA325

GET READY TO BUILD A PIPELINE OF PRIVATE MONEY!

Works Cited

[i] Crippen, S. *"Warren Buffett's $3 Billion Goldman Anniversary."* www.CNBC.com, 2009.
[ii] 2009. <http://www.squidoo.com/benjaminfranklin>.
[iii] Hill, Napoleon. The Laws of Success in Sixteen Lessons, Ralston University Press, 1928.
[iv] Covey, Stephen R. The Seven Habits of Highly Effective People. Free Press, 1989.
[v] Matthew 25:14-30
[vi] Farrel, Paul. "Warren Buffett: America's Greatest Storyteller." www.marketwatch.com. 2009.
[vii] Newsweek. January 21, 2002
[viii] 2009. <www.CNNMoney.com>.
[ix] Lenzner, Robert. "Bernie Madoff's $50 Billion Ponzi Scheme." www.forbes.com. 2009.
[x] Randolph, Keith. "Sport Visualizations." http://www.llewellyn.com/encyclopedia/article/244. 2009.
[xi] Kennedy, Dan. No B.S. Wealth Attraction for Entrepreneurs. Entrepreneur Press, 2006.
[xii] 2009. Wright, David. "Build Your Set Up From the Ground Up." http://www.wright-balance.com/tips/index.php?article=92>.
[xiii] Stanley, T. and Danko, W. The Millionaire Next Door. Simon & Schuster, 1996.
[xiv] 2009. <http://www.sec.gov/answers/accred.htm>.
[xv] 2009. <http://www.sec.gov/info/smallbus/qasbsec.htm>.
[xvi] 2009. <http://www.berkshirehathaway.com/owners.html>.
[xvii] 2009. <http://www.sba.gov/smallbusinessplanner/plan/getready/SERV_S20BPLANNER_ISENTFORU.html>.